History tells of books that connected a generation of believers to God in a transformational way. *Pilgrim's Progress* by John Bunyan, and *Mere Christianity* y C.S. Lewis, are examples of books that changed a culture. I believe that Iain and Clare Bradbeer's, *The Operating System of Jesus*, is just such a book. Using the timely analogy of computer operating systems, Iain and Clare unveil how many of us have, like Adam and Eve, opted into the self-consuming judgment of the Tree of the Knowledge of Good and Evil and opted out of the freedom won for us by Jesus- the Tree of Life.

This book is an axe to the root of the former and an urgent invitation to live and love grafted in to the fruit-bearing Tree of Life. Be prepared to find the power and the presence of a loving God in the pages of this book.

-David Noroña, Writer, Producer

As I read the pages of *The Operating System of Jesus*, I felt tangible shifts take place in my perception, mindset, and connection with God. I have literally experienced a fresh illumination of love and life with Jesus, the Tree of Life. Iain and Clare Bradbeer articulate with exceptional clarity and brilliant simplicity, the revelation of oneness and connection with Father God. While reading this book, I was enamored with childlike trust, vivid spiritual encounters, and revelatory ideas about what is possible in/with God because I am fully connected to Him. This book carries a living refreshing freedom that I have been craving to experience more. The power of the presence of God in this book has clearly transformed my life.

-Dr. Heather Ridnour, Sport Performance Psychologist

The Operating System of Jesus is outrageously brilliant and shockingly refreshing. This book is so rich. I read some of the pages over and over until I had absorbed them deeply.

Iain and Clare urge us away from the Operating System of Judgment, the legacy we have all inherited from the Tree of the Knowledge of Good and Evil. They invite us to live, instead, from the Tree of Life, a life totally connected to God's voice, His heart, His power, and His freedom.

I am so grateful to Iain and Clare Bradbeer for revealing the Truth to my previously tired and broken heart of religion. I found answers to questions that I had not let myself acknowledge I had. This book is a road map and a drink from the Tree of Life. I passionately recommend embarking on the journey of reading this book. Become you, designed by God, produced by the Holy Spirit. Breathe life in, and exhale the Operating System of Judgment out. Dare to be free.

-Diane Venora, Actress

I have known Iain and Clare for a long time. They live what they teach and their lives are a demonstration of the manifest presence of God and His nature.

This book clears a tangle of vines that have been allowed to grow over our cultural understanding of God. With kindness and strength Iain and Clare unmask structures that for too long have injured Christian people, and obscured God from the planet.

This book offers a profound pathway to peace. The reader is placed with God at the start of a pathway of life. The Authors allude to a destination, but ultimately and most profoundly, they are releasing an invitation from God, to let Him be the author and the one through whom people live. The result will be that God is seen as He is among us, and our lives will be held in His peace.

This book will change the way you think and how you operate. I was totally captivated as I turned each page.

-Tim Eldridge
Senior Leader, Harrogate New Life Church

The Operating System of Jesus is a book that expands reality as you read it. It is impossible for me to write a small number of words about something that has introduced me to possibility so vast. This is a book about the most important territory of all, the intimate places in the heart and the possibility for that space in us to be seamlessly joined to the One who loved us first. But it is so much more than that. The authors take us back to the very start, to reveal the mysteries of what happened in the Garden of Eden, and why, even today, it affects us in ways we haven't been able to see. You'll be full of hope, as I was, reading this Spirit-filled strategy to reconnect. Let every word sink in, and let love rewrite what you've believed about yourself, the world around you, and God.

-Steffany Gretzinger, Singer/Songwriter

IAIN AND CLARE BRADBEER

The power of the presence of God in this book has clearly transformed my life.

Dr. Heather Ridnour

THE OPERATING SYSTEM OF JESUS

A profoundly kind spiritual awakening

Cover Design Implementation: Robert Schwendenmann
Interior Design and Formatting: Julie Mustard
Revising and Editing: Julie Mustard
ISBN: **1499281188**

*Please note that the author's publishing style capitalizes certain pronouns in
Scripture that refer to Father, Son, and Holy Spirit and may differ from other
publishers' styles.*

TABLE OF CONTENTS

ABOUT THE AUTHORS---------------------------------- viii

INTRODUCTION-- ix

CHAPTER 1- TIME FOR A NEW OPERATING SYSTEM   1

CHAPTER 2- REDISCOVERING JESUS- THE TREE OF LIFE   17

CHAPTER 3- OUR GODLIKENESS- WITH OR WITHOUT HIM   43

CHAPTER 4- THE DESIRE FOR ONENESS   58

CHAPTER 5- JESUS DEFEATED JUDGMENT   64

CHAPTER 6- CHOOSE JESUS, NOT JUDGMENT   81

CHAPTER 7- LOVE ENCOUNTERS ANCHOR US   86

CHAPTER 8- BELIEF MUST COME ALIVE   91

CHAPTER 9- JESUS IS LIVING TRUTH   98

CHAPTER 10- BREAKING FREE FROM JUDGMENT   105

CHAPTER 11- JESUS' COMMUNICATION   127

CHAPTER 12- A NEW EMOTIONAL LANDSCAPE   153

CHAPTER 13- CASTING FRESH LIGHT ON THE BIBLE   170

CHAPTER 14- BRIEF OVERVIEW OF THE BIBLE   174

CHAPTER 15- THE RICH YOUNG RULER   189

CHAPTER 16- NOT JUST JUDGMENT-FREE   197

CHAPTER 17- GETTING REAL WITH GOD   205

CHAPTER 18- WHAT IS THE FAITH LIFE?   212

CHAPTER 19- LIVING UNOFFENDED   217

CHAPTER 20- INHABITING PEACE   222

CHAPTER 21- THE PLANET GETS TO SEE GOD AS HE IS   238

ABOUT THE AUTHORS

Born into the humanity of small town church life, Iain grew up the son of a Presbyterian minister. Iain moved to Melbourne at the age of 11 when his father became Chaplain at Scotch College, a school with a student population larger than the entire town he left.

Iain went on to study Architecture and Construction Management, eventually managing his own residential practice in Melbourne. Clare studied both Family and Occupational Therapy, working predominately in long-term case management in community based mental health programs.

Their shared intuition has given them their great ability to shift people from culturally or intellectually inherited disconnection into deep and transformational access to God. Iain travels internationally speaking and teaching and consulting leaders across a variety of fields.

Both Iain and Clare love to process the deep issues of life with God and one another as they do life with their three sons and one Wheaten Terrier in Melbourne, Australia.

INTRODUCTION

As an editor, I usually distance myself from feeling or experiencing the book I am working on. After all, mine is the technical task of applying my skills to release the work into the fullest expression of itself- it is never about me. Like many books before, I planned to approach this work, *The Operating System of Jesus*, with certain objectivity, an objectivity that allows me to get my job done well.

That approach didn't work this time.

As I began to read the first chapter, my spirit began to stir. I saw places and felt realities that I had longed for, but never dared to believe could be mine. With each turn of the page, I was invited deeper into connection with the Author of Life.

The Author of Life has always been my friend, but much like editing a book, structures of human limitation can be used to author alternate realities that God, by nature, cannot inhabit. We edit Him out of "normal" human life by tradition, even when our desire would be the complete opposite if only we could see.

With each chapter of the book, my spirit moved further away from places of limitation into free and open places with God. I had 1,000 questions, and I asked Iain and Clare all of them. They would respond with simple provocations back to the deep place, the place in me that was really ready to live, ready to become the fullest expression of me, authored by a God who is more available, more real, and more able than I dared to let myself hope. In the kindest, gentlest way, these authors, the profoundly sensitive friends of God, refused to give me what I wanted, simple answers that I could use to edit God out of my life. Instead, they would tell my heart to stay in the new territory, the new expanse of openness, until I learned to be at home in a big place with an unlimited God.

With every strikethrough of my false beliefs, my rewrites of truth, and wording changes in my heart and mind, something beautiful in me became very clear: the reality of my union with God and my personal heart-connection to The Author of Life. I found Us, Him, and me together in every sentence of this book.

As you embark on the journey through it, enter with courage and belief that He is jealous for you – all of you. This isn't a weekend read or a book to check off a list. It is a book that will shatter prison gates and open wide the doors of the human heart.

~Julie Mustard
Editor

Chapter 1

TIME FOR A NEW OPERATING SYSTEM

Operating systems define exactly what computer technology will do for people. Pre-installed and activated at the first push of the power button, every functioning moment of a computer-controlled device is governed by its operating system. The invention of the computer operating system provided a foundational software platform that could direct and prioritize multiple functions for multiple users. Behind the scenes, operating systems are now a quintessential part of modern life.

In this book, we borrow the term "operating system" to open up a new perspective on mankind's greatest opportunity: The opportunity to know God.

God designed an operating system for people that puts us in direct and perceptible connection to Him and holds us there. It is a way of living that trains our senses into an awareness of God so that we can choose to live moment by moment in response to what He is doing. It is the way Jesus lived, *"The Son can do nothing of Himself, but what He sees the Father do; for whatever He does, the Son also does in like manner"* (John 5:19). It makes God's infinite ability and wisdom available to us in the activities of daily life. This operating system is centered on a strong connection to God causing everything a person does or says to become an expression of the connection. Step by step, through this connection, we are empowered beyond normal human limits. God's infinite ability enables His best plans to come to life through us. As we adopt this operating system, our lives become compelling demonstrations of the God who is with us.

This operating system, which we call "the Operating System of Jesus," is the opportunity to live the way Jesus did. It is the way of eternal life. Completely secure, directly and constantly connected to God's love, purposes, and power, this operating system takes us from strength to strength. It is not a set of rules. It is not a contractual arrangement. It is the living reality of being with God, and that reality comes alive to the planet around us as we do the things God has for us to do and speak the words He has for us to say. Miracles, wisdom, love, hope and inspiration are great treasures of the Infinite One that are delivered into "normal" life through us as we become God's friends. The possibility for this way of living, God's original plan for Mankind, was represented in the Garden of Eden by the Tree of Life, a prophetic picture of Jesus (Genesis 2:9).

Jesus confounded the leaders of His time when He displayed how life looked under His operating system. His system took instruction from a different "source code," one of limitless possibility. The Pharisees and lawmakers of His day recognized it as incompatible with the code they based their lives on. They found his healing of a withered hand on the Sabbath confronting and started plotting how they could use Jesus' non-compliance to bring Him down. Jesus usurped their legal offence, posing this question: "*I will ask you one thing: Is it lawful on the Sabbath to do good or to do evil, to save life or to destroy?*" (Luke 6:9) Jesus was showing them that the complex code they were under had become a barrier to true goodness and life.

> *This operating system, which we call "the operating system of Jesus," is the opportunity to live the way Jesus did. It is the way of eternal life.*

Jesus confounded the political expectations of His time. Many Jews wanted a military campaign to free them from Roman rule, but the freedom Jesus offered them came without military or political revolution. His relationship with Father God was not the set of behaviors and constraints they believed was necessary; instead, it seemed to produce one catalytic comment or action after another. Jesus was indefinable and irresistible. He had the power to create anything and the ability to understand everything; His life was the ultimate code break into infinite possibility. All attempts to undermine Jesus or disempower Him failed. Jesus came with such authority that legions of dark powers fled when He spoke. The way Jesus did things was effective without positional authority, social status, or professional association. The greatness at work in Him was recognizable across every social strata and, most importantly, in the spirit realm.

Enter Judgment

The Operating System of Jesus was inserted by God into the context of a human civilization that had written its history with the use of a very different operating system. In the Garden of Eden, right back at the very beginning, the Operating System of Judgment was activated when the serpent tricked Eve. He scared her. He speculated about God's intentions, and in doing so, caused her to question within herself, and "helped" her take matters into her own hands. The devil severely undermined Eve's attachment to God. In her vulnerability, Eve decided to navigate herself.

The main tool humans use for navigating through life is judgment, the practice of evaluating evidence to make decisions. Judgments are made from our own power to study, observe, consider, and process inputs. Judgment is a complex tool. It makes us feel equipped and able, but the limitations and constraints it creates remain undiscovered initially. Judgment makes an individual the director of their own life; they become responsible for success or failure. By operating under a system of judgment, a person is acting as his or her own godhead. Judgment structures the living God out and puts us in His place.

Adam and Eve introduced the world to what this book calls, *"the Operating System of Judgment."* What started with one decision, one instance of judgment, ended mankind's access to a life of simple communion with God. From that moment forward, humans began to navigate life through judgment-based decisions, instead of a life of direct communion with God. The story that describes this devastating deviation away from God is the story of Adam and Eve and the Tree of the Knowledge of Good and Evil (Genesis 3). When Adam and Eve put their faith in their own judgments, they began the transition of a whole civilization into a new way of life completely founded on human judgment. Over the millennia, humans have amassed a wealth of information, perceptions, and paradigms that we collectively call, "reality." Thousands of years later, the Operating System of Judgment holds people captive to this collective human-judgment-based "reality."

> *Most people have unknowingly been trained into navigating through life using the Operating System of Judgment. It was never designed for us.*

Most people have unknowingly been trained into navigating through life using the Operating System of Judgment. It was never designed for us. It is the way of directing human life that positions us within limits and constraints, shuts down our ability to hear and see God, and binds us into time in a way that steals from our present. It is an unseen foundation that keeps people out of close and intimate union with God. Under judgment, people are required to judge, assess, consider, and make decisions from inside of their own abilities. People become the director and the ultimate reference point for everything we think and do. Without the anchor of attachment to God, the actively demonstrated spiritual authority of an individual is the intrinsic power of their own spirit. We were not designed to be that vulnerable.

The Operating System of Judgment has blocked the planet's access to God, but most people are unaware that Jesus came to deliver us out of it. We can opt out of this inherited system and learn how to live the operating system modeled by Jesus. His life on earth was a demonstration of this new way, the representation of God's original idea: God and people living in spiritual connection, in complete union. Jesus' operating system is every bit as available to us now as it was to Him. The Holy Spirit is God's gift to empower us in this way of life. This book removes the barriers and helps trade in the old operating system for one that leads to a constant, life-giving connection to God. Jesus died to make this possible for us.

The Light

Jesus did not die to lead us into a life of Christian ideas, awkward constraint, pressure, or uncertainty. He lived His life directly out of the substance of God, the very substance available to us. Jesus said, *"You are the light of the world"* when addressing a group of people (Matthew 5:14, John 8:12). He challenged people to live from this place and not hide or assess, saying, *"Nor do they light a lamp and put it under a bushel, but on a lamp stand, and it gives light to all* who are *in the house"* (Matthew 5:15). A bushel was a jug or container used to measure volume. Jesus shows that the bushel, an assessment tool, could destroy the effectiveness of God's supernatural light. Similarly, God's effect in us and through us is limited if we put Him under the Operating System of Judgment.

> **Beliefs and ideas about God are not the same as having God.**

The Operating System of Judgment is mutually exclusive from the life-giving and manifest reality of God. When a person learns the Operating System of Jesus, it is easy for God to display Himself to them and through them. Jesus taught that all of the people who are "*the light*" are assembled into "*a city on a hill that cannot be hidden*" (Matthew 5:14). The reality of God's presence in His people becomes obvious and practically available throughout the world. It all starts with the simplicity of a real and living inhabitation of one person by God. In the words of Jesus, "*If anyone loves Me, he will keep My words. My Father will love him, and We will come to him and make Our home with him*" (John 14:23). The word "**keep**" is used to translate the Greek word *tēreō* which is more fully expressed as "to attend to carefully" or "to take care of." Our careful reverence for the living voice of God will lead to the same personal connection with The Father that Jesus had.

Christians are encouraged to express the idea that they have a personal relationship with God. However, many live with very little, if any, sense of the connection to Him. Washed haplessly from decade to decade in a river of effort and theological speculation, believers are asked to overlook disappointment. If people want greater certainty, they take some sort of stance, forming a lifetime commitment to a set of beliefs because people have not known how to live out every day with God Himself. Beliefs and ideas about God are not the same as having God. Knowing how to know God has been veiled by our corporate complicity with a system of judgment- a life of relationships marked by an abundance of ideas and beliefs about Him and limited or momentary access to His power or presence.

The uncertainty many people attribute to a life of faith in God is an expression of the disconnection caused by trying to have a relationship with God using an operating system that separates us from Him. Jesus never said He would *sometimes* be with us, and all the other times we would just have to trust our own determination, hold onto "*the promises*," and wait for the season to shift. Jesus promised He would *always* be with us, and never leave us (Matthew 28:20; Hebrews 13:5). From the beginning, it was God's desire that He would be *Emmanuel,* the God who lives in and with His people (Matthew 1:23).

The Christian life is not supposed to be an uncertain and insecure walk of unfulfilled ideas about God. Neither is it to be based on speculation about what God wants us to do to represent Him well. Jesus was never insecure. He represented the Father perfectly, not because He knew so much that He could always figure out the right thing to do, but because Jesus was never disconnected from God. Everything He did was a direct demonstration of what the Father wanted to make happen on the earth in that moment. He showed the Father's power and nature directed through Jesus to destroy the works of evil around Him and establish the things Father God wanted established. His connection to Father God was to enable the demonstration of the Father's nature and the Father's resurrection power. Jesus promised that like Him, we too, never need to be disconnected.

> *The Christian life is not supposed to be an uncertain and insecure walk of unfulfilled ideas about God.*

Systemic Deception

For many people, the minimal connection they have with God is a very painful subject. The solution has always been introspection and a pressure for personal growth, based on the premise that something is "wrong" with them. In this book, we are uncovering a huge trick that has sidelined much of the history of mankind out of the direct flow of the life of God. This has been a global systemic deception.

The Operating System of Judgment, where we consider, review, assess, and judge to decide the "best" way forward, is so familiar to modern people that they believe it is an intrinsic part of being human. It is assumed that a life of faith in God is overlaid on top of that foundation; however, operating out of judgment is not intrinsic to being human. It is very harmful. It is, in fact, the use of a navigational tool that consigns us to live out of our own God-likeness without a living connection to God. It is a choice that most people don't realize they have agreed to make because the deception has been buried as an invisible foundation under all of our lives.

At a civilizational level, everything around us reinforces the "value" of this way of living and no individual within that ecosystem thinks they have a choice to live any other way. But God never intended for us to govern ourselves separate from Him, or "in His name" void of any real sense of Him. God never intended us to have to navigate something as complex as life without Him. He never wanted us to have to live inside the reduced realities and assumptions we must make to guide ourselves within the Operating System of Judgment. The Operating System of Jesus and the Operating System of Judgment are mutually exclusive.

> *The operating system of Jesus and the Operating System of Judgment are mutually exclusive.*

Christianity was never meant to be a roadmap for a lifetime of biblically-based self-governance. We have missed seeing an operating system where humanity became self-directed and, therefore, constrained in our ability to know God. Eve activated the Operating System of Judgment; Jesus disarmed it. Unfortunately, we reactivate it when we operate out of judgment. In this book, we shine light on this operating system and unmask its anchor points so that we can shed it and step into life with the God who is very near.

Proverbs 3:5-6

I lived for years by my understanding of the English translation of Proverbs 3:5-6. It reads, *"Trust in the Lord with all your heart and do not lean on your own understanding. In all your ways acknowledge God and He will make your paths straight."*

The Hebrew reads: "batach YHVH leb sha'an biynah derek yada' yashar 'orach." The first word "batach" suggests *a strong and confident quality, or a strength of habitation.* This "trust" is not hesitant or tentative, it is absolute certitude. The problem though, in our understanding, begins with the word "Yada." This word has been cleaned-up for palatability in translation. In Hebrew, the word is used to describe sexual "knowing," an intense and unmediated union, oneness. Because of translation, we have lost the fullness of its invitation to have an intimate and personal union with the One who is without beginning and without end, Yahweh or Jehovah. In place of that, we have taken on the burden of "acknowledging Him" in the right ways.

Once we are invited into "yada," this scripture then contrasts union with the alternative that is not recommended - the way of our own understanding. It is the operating system Eve adopted when she chose to operate outside of oneness with

God. This is what we call "the Operating System of Judgment." Retranslated as a prophetic description of the operating system Jesus came to introduce, this scripture says, *"Be confident and strong, positioned inside the Eternal One, rather than living from your own understanding. Union with God positions you to be directed by Him in the way."*

The Way

Throughout the Old Testament, we are pointed toward this comprehensively transformed lifestyle in God. Since Jesus described Himself as "The Way," the scripture could be translated to mean, "Live confident and from union with God rather than from what you understand. Union with God is the way of Jesus." Divine union causes our life to become a living tribute to Jesus. Our own understanding of the "right" way to make our "path straight" will always lead us away from the union with God that we are actually seeking.

It is now two thousand years since Jesus showed us God's intended way, but the Operating System of Judgment, like a persistent weed, still flourishes, disguising itself as the normal Christian life. Believers are taught into it. This operating system causes Christian believers pain, marginalization, and bewilderment. The purpose of Jesus' life on earth was *not* to establish a group linked by a set of beliefs about God. We were not supposed to be people who, because we believed certain things, lived and behaved certain ways to demonstrate those beliefs. Rather, as children of God adopted by a heavenly Father, we get to fulfill the desire of Jesus, *"that they also may be one in Us, that the world may believe that You sent Me"* (John 17:21).

This is the active, moment-by-moment connection to God; we manifest aspects of Him as we do and say the exact things that reveal His living nature to the world around us—miracles of healing, words we speak that unlock problems, reveal God's heart for His children and the planet, or wisdom that makes a way when there seems to be none. Living from our connection to God, doing and saying what the Father has for us to do and say, is a life of knowing and experiencing God's absolute nearness. This Operating System of Jesus, the Tree of Life, was God's plan for us from the beginning.

> *We are invited to hear His voice, think His thoughts, and speak His words.*

When we know how to do what the Father is doing, great things are possible. One day, I was ordering lunch with a friend when he quietly asked the waitress if she had back pain. "Why?" she asked. My friend told her that Jesus had just walked by him, and he had watched Jesus go to her and touch her back. The waitress twisted around a bit and confirmed that the chronic pain in her back was completely gone. Jesus is alive and with us and that healing was what He wanted done in that moment at that restaurant. My friend knew how to partner with what God was doing. The planet wants God. It is time for people to discover the security of being attached to Him and the pleasure of being direct conduits of Him. We long to live into the full transformational opportunity of Jesus' life, death, and resurrection. We do not want a "Jesus-themed life" or to be playing some kind of hit-or-miss spiritual sport with a God who apparently loves us but is barely available. His operating system, the way Jesus showed us how to live, means that the world will be able to say of us what Jesus said of Himself, that "He who has seen Me has seen the Father" (John 14:9).

Jesus invites us to know a God who is generous and tender, to come into a deep and profound communion with Him. We are invited to hear His voice, think His thoughts, and speak His words. We are God's nominated home. Our bodies are designed to house Him. Through Jesus, it is possible to be an extension of God Himself. We are to "eat His flesh" and "drink His blood" (John 6:56) and together, as a family of "beloved children" (John 1:12), do the "greater works" (John 14:12) Jesus told us we would do.

Empowering individual believers to walk in intimate connection with God would make possible a church that could give the world a clear revelation of the Father. Every day on this planet, "normal life" could be punctuated by millions of "acts of God," designed by Him and delivered through His children. Every time one of these works of His goodness happens, things change. Life and hope and love win. Hell is put to shame. Many people are coming out of jails created by the Operating System of Judgment and into the intimate and sustained relationship with Father God that is the foundation of the Operating System of Jesus.

Encountering Introspection

A friend shared a dream, "*I saw myself laid out on an operating table surrounded by surgeons wearing masks and gowns. Some were familiar faces, others not. They were taking out my organs, examining them, cleaning and replacing some, and discarding others. There was immense purpose in the room. I watched them, completely absorbed in their craft; assembling a beautiful new city inside me.*

My satisfaction was interrupted by a whisper, "Where is Jesus?" I looked down past the end of the operating table and saw Him there watching. He was standing still and in pain. Suddenly, I lost my numbness and felt immense pain. I caught onto why Jesus was angry. I asked Him the question "Did you put me on this table?" He answered with tender quietness but with much anger towards the surgery going on in the room. "No," He said, "I was laid out on that table so that you wouldn't have to be." Jesus took a step towards the table and the surgeons lowered their heads and walked away.

God gave me a lifeline that day. Until then, I had believed that offering myself up for improvement meant that I was humble, accountable, and teachable. Instead of going from strength to strength and glory to glory, I had entered a lifestyle of self-condemnation and striving. Each time, the challenge was this: Would I give Jesus all of me? I had committed to being as critique-able as required in my church life, but privately, I just moved forward as best I could.

Everything changed in that operating suite. All of the accusation, and welcomed critique became accountable to Jesus. I really had no idea that Jesus came to set us free from judgment, but He did."

Living from our connection to God, doing and saying what the Father has for us to do and say, is a life of knowing and experiencing God's absolute nearness.

The teaching and application that follows in this book will help you:

> •Have a revelation of the full opportunity that Jesus' life on earth gave you to be a child of God, attached to Him, and accessing that connection in every situation.

•See how the Operating System of Judgment has woven itself through every sphere of human endeavor, restricting our connection to God, causing pain and marginalization, and creating conflict as people everywhere are forced to navigate life with minimal access to God.

•Activate the Operating System of Jesus in your own life so that you can live out of your connection to God and leave the constricted life under the Operating System of Judgment behind.

•Start the journey into unlimited knowing of God, releasing yourself into the plans and ideas that God has in mind for you. This is the life of connection with God where His nature is free to manifest through you, and the fruit of your life is as much divine as it is human.

Dietrich Bonhoeffer, a German theologian, taught that man was meant to be positioned fully one with God and that everything a person thinks, feels, and does is supposed to be from that oneness. In His writings in 1943, which were compiled into the book, *Ethics*, Bonhoeffer commented that the practice of a person deciding one way or another actually indicated an existing separation from God. He stated that man ideally should be operating in complete union with God and should not be in a position to "know" anything without that union as the reference point of all knowledge. Bonhoeffer said, "Man at his origin knows only one thing: God. It is only in the unity of his knowledge of God that he knows of other men, of things and of himself. He knows all things only in God and God in all things" (Bonhoeffer 18). What we refer to as union with God or connection with God, Bonhoeffer calls being "at the origin."

It is time for the world to see a tribe of believers, billions strong, all confident of God's mercy and goodness, all with a history of hearing His living voice and being a direct conduit between God and the details of life on this planet. We must stop "trying" to represent God in the "right" way without any real connection that directly manifests His nature. The fruit of God from the life of today's believer has the potential to reveal God in a measure that will call whole nations into His goodness and then into the freedom of living in and from God. This is the kind of freedom that builds righteousness. We will be confident as the living God delivers, through us, what the planet longs for.

> *We must stop "trying" to represent God in the "right" way without any real connection that directly manifests His nature.*

Accessing the Tree of Life

So how does the Operating System of Jesus, The Tree of Life, get established in our lives?

Living in the Operating System of Jesus requires a radical deliverance from the Operating System of Judgment and the spiritual jails that it has created. Being grafted into God and living out the Operating System of Jesus feels and looks fundamentally different than that jail. A new foundation in God must be built. We must go to the origin of the constraining mechanisms that the majority of people live under and uproot it.

John the Baptist told us that he had come to *"put an axe to the roots of the tree."* John the Baptist was sent to break people free from the legacy of the Tree of the Knowledge of Good and

Evil and awaken us to our opportunity to eat from the One who is the Tree of Life, Jesus (Genesis 2:16; John 6:55). We don't need to become reformers who advocate improvements to existing Christian institutions or cultures around us. What we do need is a new understanding of God's original idea for mankind and how to eat from the Tree of Life, Jesus, so that our lives become a living display of His best plans.

Chapter 2

REDISCOVERING JESUS – THE TREE OF LIFE

The Bible draws attention to two particular trees in the Garden of Eden- The Tree of the Knowledge of Good and Evil and the Tree of Life. Studies of "the fall" of mankind historically turn more attention toward the Tree of the Knowledge of Good and Evil and its role in Mankind's journey away from God than to the Tree of Life. Because we feel

> *The cost to the planet of this obsession with avoiding "doing the wrong thing" is very great.*

compelled to try to avoid doing "wrong," Adam and Eve's mistake in the Garden of Eden has become our corporate focus.

People assume our job is to study the Bible to find out how to get it "right" where so many others, like Eve, have failed. The cost to the planet of this obsession with avoiding "doing the wrong thing" has been very great. Because we haven't enquired deeply into the centrality of the Tree of Life, we have overlooked what God hoped and provided for us from the very beginning - an unimaginably good opportunity to take into ourselves His very nature and become people who live in eternal and indivisible connection with Him. Consequently, we have vast collective resources dedicated to "getting it right" and applying the "correct" biblical overlay to whatever area of life we are focused on, and a paucity of leaders, teachers, books, and role models that advocate and teach people into connection with the living God Himself.

The Tree of Life

Jesus is the Tree of Life. We are told that this tree stood in the very center of the Garden of Eden (Genesis 2:9). Adam and Eve were invited to eat from it, that is, to make what it had to offer a part of their lives. God's desire was that we would join ourselves to the Tree of Life, and navigate all of life in union with Him into eternity. If Adam and Eve had continued in the Operating System of Jesus, eating from the Tree of Life, their lives would not have been constrained by the natural world. Completely in sync with God, they would have lived forever.

Jump forward to Proverbs, in the middle of the Bible, and the Tree of Life appears again. Proverbs 13:12: *"Hope deferred makes the heart sick, but when the desire comes, it is a tree of life."* In other words, God's deferred hope, His longing for intimate and personal connection to mankind, which had been lost by the activation of a judgment-based operating system, would be fulfilled one day by Jesus, the Savior, who is the Tree of Life. The Tree of Life appears three more times in Revelation, the very last book of the Bible (Revelation 22:2). Here, it is the tree in the very center of the Heavenly City, the tree described as fruitful in every season.

Jesus and His redemptive opportunity is the absolute focus of God. The fruitfulness in every season is a demonstration of how the Tree of Life operates in us to release God and His life-giving power, no matter the circumstances around us. The whole Bible is held between these images of the Tree of Life, at the beginning, middle, and end. This revelation of Jesus, the Tree of Life, is our opportunity to live into oneness with God.

> *The fruitfulness in every season is a demonstration of how the Tree of Life operates in us to release God.*

Valuing the prophetic picture of the Tree of Life and understanding how it represents God's redemptive heart opens up deeper revelation of Jesus Himself from parts of Scripture we may already be familiar with. For example, John 3:16 is the treasured verse that celebrates the Father heart of God and His sending of Jesus to restore the opportunity for us to have direct and effective connection with God. Many are familiar with the English translation that says, "*For God so loved the world that He gave His only begotten Son, that whosoever believes in Him should not perish but have everlasting life.*" In English-speaking Christian tradition, this scripture is almost universally taken to mean, "If I believe in a God called Jesus and believe that He died on the cross, as it says in the Bible, and believe the right ideas about Him, then I will go to heaven when I die." This idea of "believe in" is, "I subscribe to a story," "I accept a story as a true account," or "I have decided to accept as true that Jesus is the Savior of the universe, and that, by believing this, I will get to heaven."

A more faithful rendering of the original Greek text would be: "Those who trust Jesus and *fully give themselves into Him*, those who transition their life from outside of Him to inside of Him, will die to the way of death and be married to the One who is without beginning and without end." This language asks for a much fuller giving of one's whole self, a much stronger "all of life" connection and unending reward. This level of reward, "entering into a marriage-like union with Jesus," is very hard to wrap our minds around.

Our normal English translation of John 3:16 implies that "eternal life" is some kind of place or state that one goes to after a person dies, *IF* that person fulfilled the criteria. In the paraphrase above, I have suggested that it is instead a "way" that starts now and involves an experience of reality marked by access to the infinite nature of God. It is a "way" of living that is impossible under the Operating System of Judgment which is defined by limits that are structured in by judgment. Instead, eternal life is our opportunity to come into union with the infinite potential of God who is without limit and without end; that opportunity can be accessed now.

Beyond the Structure

God exists beyond the reaches of any paradigm (set of ideas that structure human understanding). In choosing to access union with Him now, we choose to leave behind the limits that would define reality under the Operating System of Judgment. Union with God gives us access to wisdom and understanding otherwise inconceivable from within "normal" human thinking. Most people only see inside the paradigm they are taught or choose to inhabit.

In positioning our minds with God, we think from beyond any system or limitation and bring what we find there, in the unconstrained, infinite realms of God, back into day-to-day life. Scholars often assume that when we explore a new hypothesis we must suspend an area of presupposition so that we can discover new information. Western thinking accepts that some version of this reductionary process must accompany all exploration and discovery. Such thinking assumes that every human situation is defined or limited by its context.

But, God is the infinite One; He exists beyond limits and is Himself the context maker. He cannot be accurately represented when contained within limits of human devising. With access to God, people too can be free, as Jesus was, to join God in "thinking" from His realm, without the limits of paradigms. This was part of God's original plan for humans. He wanted us to be able to access Him fully. That means access to wisdom, information, and solutions to problems

20

beyond what we can resolve from our human journey. Jesus showed us what it looked like to operate with this infinite ability.

The Samaritan woman was changed by this very thing she encountered in Jesus (John 4:7-29). Jesus' connection to God gave Him supernatural knowledge of her personal history that opened this woman, and many in her town, to a complete change of life. This relational flow of God's wisdom and knowledge can be used by God to achieve a particular outcome whenever He chooses. It is important to remember that Jesus was constrained by being "fully human;" a human just like us.

He willingly constrained His godhead to work within the form of a human life that was completely yielded to the Father. Because He never established a barrier to His connection to God through sin or judgment, Jesus' life was an unimpeded demonstration of Father God. His hearing from God and knowing God was not an exclusive divine power. He was demonstrating the way He knew how to live out the human journey.

He knew at the end of His earthly life He would set up the opportunity for us to be able to live this way. We are able to learn how to listen to God, to know Him, and to live out of that knowing just as Jesus did.

> *Jesus demonstrated how to live out human connection to God so we could live this way also.*

Christine's Story

One day, I was having coffee with a mother of three teenage girls. It was the first time I had met her, so I did not know anything about her or her family. The conversation started relatively light, but just as I thought we were finishing up, God painted a picture across my field of vision. It was a cross-section through a flat inland region, coastal mountains, and the coastline. Water was coming from an underground storage and bubbling up in what I somehow knew to be the woman's backyard. I also saw water being bottled and loaded into trucks and distributed. I told the woman what I saw, and my sense that an inland aquifer was becoming a resource in her backyard and that she was going to become a resource to the whole nation through this. I had no idea whether God was speaking literally, metaphorically, or both.

She then revealed that she and her husband were in a "David and Goliath" battle with a very large beverage company over commercial rights to an underground spring. At that moment, because of the picture I shared with her, she was encouraged to continue with the effort because she heard from a source that was beyond her "natural" limits. She heard from God.

The opportunity to connect with God, and speak and do things that come directly from Him, is the supernatural opportunity to live beyond paradigm. A contemporary focus on "the supernatural" reflects a hunger for our union with God to manifest in a moment-by-moment expression of what God the Father wants to do through us. It is not "the supernatural" that is our goal; rather, that the Children of God be a free and empowered conduit of His nature instead of an unfortunate display of the limits and harm produced by the Operating System of Judgment.

No matter which emphasis we choose, supernatural, academic, or any mixture in between, if the emphasis is chosen by us and anchored into assumption, assessment, or judgment, the Operating System of Judgment will limit, filter and distort God's expression through us. As children of God, we can and must live from our connection with the Infinite One.

Our connection to God becomes a direct bridge between God's infinite nature and the "finite" natural world. Jesus was the first human to operate from outside the paradigms created by the Operating System of Judgment and live in constant access to God. He modeled this for us so we could do likewise. He was "begotten" and we are "adopted" (Galatians 4:4-7; Ephesians 1:5). We are all sons and daughters and Scripture is clear that we are can be like Him (Galatians 4:1-7). We have the same access He had to wisdom (1 Corinthians 2:16; (Ephesians 1:17) and resources (Ephesians 1:19) from outside the limitations of humanity. It is our family inheritance. Jesus was our model.

> *As children of God, we can and must live from our connection with the Infinite One.*

The Other Tree in the Garden

In order to see the Garden of Eden story more fully, we cannot ignore a deeper look into the Tree of the Knowledge of Good and Evil. It is extraordinarily hard to address the incident with Adam and Eve from a fresh perspective because people generally view it from the Operating System of Judgment. It is extraordinarily hard to come to this with fresh eyes because people generally grow up in the environment shaped by the Operating System of Judgment that skews our interpretation of Bible stories.

We have missed out on seeing that the Tree of the Knowledge of Good and Evil stood for an **operating system** because the Operating System of Judgment itself has restricted the way we see, perceive, and teach. Inside this operating system, our attention is distracted away from understanding what God is doing, and turned to deciding good from bad, right from wrong, and aligning ourselves with what we determine to be the best, most "correct," most appropriate, or most likely successful way forward. We note Adam and Eve's disobedience and failure to do the "right" thing, but we miss seeing the change in the operating system triggered by their actions.

The Tree of the Knowledge of Good and Evil represented the choice to navigate life as our own director. God didn't explain how eating from the Tree of the Knowledge of Good and Evil would lead to death. He just told Eve not to eat from it because doing so would cause death. If Eve would have complied with this instruction, she would have activated absolute trust in God, resulting in a demonstration that no barrier between God and people was established or empowered.

If, instead, God would have included an explanation that eating from the Tree of the Knowledge of Good and Evil would cause her to become separated from Him and have to navigate without Him, Eve could have complied with God's instruction out of self-interest. This response would also have activated her into navigating life by the Operating System of Judgment rather than childlike trust in God. Knowing this helps us to understand why God required them to obey a simple instruction not to eat from the Tree of the Knowledge of Good and Evil. The obedience had to be out of childlike trust. Obedience out of a judgment to do what was "right," or in self-preservation, would also have activated the Operating System of Judgment.

There is Hope

Before the story of Eve's interaction with the serpent, Scripture records that God strongly approved of all the created world, including the people He made. This is a foundational treasure as we position ourselves for union with Him. We are invited into life and into intimate relationship by a good Father, God, whose dominant nature is love and who is pleased with how He made us. Before we are even through the first chapter of the Bible, God makes this declaration about the cosmos: *"Then God saw everything that He had made, and indeed it was very good"* (Genesis 1:31). From the very outset, God was delighted with people and the planet. Knowing this is vital. Everything about our approach to God changes because we know that He likes us.

I grew up thinking God may be good but people are not, and Eve proved it by choosing the Tree of the Knowledge of Good and Evil. Such an accusation and assumption is a very useful way to trap a population in an endless cycle of self-assessment, condemnation, and God-themed self-improvement. This level of accusation, that people are not good, is both an expression and a cause of disordered attachment. Attachment disorder is a feature of cultures built by an operating system that disconnects people from God; accusations of this nature towards people are not biblical and not supported by the life or actions of Jesus.

> *There is nothing in Scripture telling us that Eve, prior to her conversation with the serpent, had any inclination to disobey God.*

God made mankind and declared a *blessing* over us. He said that we were *"very good."* If Eve was less than good, what would that say about God? That He was lying? That He did not really know Eve? If her failure to obey was a demonstration that she was flawed, then God's assessment of His creation was wrong. But God cannot be wrong, and mankind is, as He declared, very good.

Pressure from an external source (Satan) was required to set Eve off track. She was, like her maker, designed to operate in goodness. The serpent had to pressure and trick Eve. There is nothing in the Scripture that tells us that Eve, prior to her conversation with the serpent, had any inclination to disobey God. If her nature had been flawed then this inclination would have come from within her. Instead, the devil needed to come as an external source of pressure to shift Eve away from the simplicity she had with God, then lead her into a relationship with judgment.

The devil was determined that he would take Eve from a full and intimate "knowing" (yada) of God into a way of navigating life based on "knowing" (yada) good and evil. The devil tricked her, and subsequently mankind, away from the fullness and unhindered relationship with God and brought people into the vulnerability of having to navigate their own way by judgment.

The Seed of Doubt

This structural shift caused so much harm. Examining the passage closely reveals what really happened:

> Genesis 3:1: *"Now the serpent was more cunning than any beast of the field which the LORD God had made. And he said to the woman, "Has God indeed said, 'You shall not eat of every tree of the garden'?" 2. And the woman said to*

> *the serpent, "We may eat the fruit of the trees of the garden;*
> *3. "but of the fruit of the tree which is in the midst of the*
> *garden, God has said, 'You shall not eat it, nor shall you*
> *touch it, lest you die.'" 4. Then the serpent said to the*
> *woman, "You will not surely die. 5. "For God knows that*
> *in the day you eat of it your eyes will be opened, and you*
> *will be like God, knowing good and evil." 6. So when the*
> *woman saw that the tree [was] good for food, that it [was]*
> *pleasant to the eyes, and a tree desirable to make [one] wise,*
> *she took of its fruit and ate. She also gave some to her*
> *husband with her, and he ate. 7. Then the eyes of both of*
> *them were opened, and they knew that they [were] naked;*
> *and they sewed fig leaves together and made themselves*
> *coverings. 8. And they heard the sound of the LORD God*
> *walking in the garden in the cool of the day, and Adam and*
> *his wife hid themselves from the presence of the LORD God*
> *among the trees of the garden."*

Here are the details of what happened to Eve. First, Satan provoked Eve to *DOUBT* God's goodness. Up to that point, Eve had no reason to doubt that God was good, not one reason to believe that God would not always be kind and generous to her or not promote her interests. The devil introduced her to these sorts of questions: Is God safe? Is He trustworthy? Could He be trying to rip me off? After discovering doubt and fear, she chose to embrace them. Eve made some sort of *JUDGMENT,* for example, that God might actually be trying to deprive her. She decided to take action to avert that possibility.

Although the Bible does not tell us exactly what she was thinking, we know that, as a minimum, she judged the devil's input to be worthwhile, thus choosing to be guided by her own judgments. Having chosen to navigate by her own judgments about the devil's suggestions, Eve took *ACTION* based on her assessment. She got Adam to eat the fruit too, and then they both made new outfits and started to hide from God. She chose to make assessments and form solutions by herself outside of her connection to God.

God's words to her were no longer her determining force. The judge in her own head was now the primary determiner of her direction. She activated herself as the operational godhead and her power to judge would now be used to navigate. This is what the Devil was talking about when he promised Eve that she would "know good and evil." Adam and Eve now had a "yada" relationship with good and evil. The devil omitted that once they had that, they would be shut out of a "yada" relationship with God.

Eve did not know she was walking away from childlike trust in God, but that's what she did. Satan gave her a way to weigh and measure her options and to consider that she might be able to take better care of herself than God. When it came time to choose, she chose to go with the option of trusting herself. It was a change of position from **with God** and **trusting God**, to **near God** and **trusting herself.** Bonhoeffer described this change as a change from God being the "origin" to us being our own "origin." *(Dietrich Bonhoeffer, MacMillan Publishing 1986 Ethics, p. 18).*

For mankind, it triggered the creation of an operating system derived from the Tree of the Knowledge of Good and Evil; a whole new way of life that was intimately entwined with judgment. Many people are taught that it was Adam and Eve's fallen (evil) nature that separated them from God. It was not a change in mankind's nature which caused the separation. The choice to activate trust in our own godlikeness without connection to God, as Eve did, keeps us separated from God the Father by compelling us to come into a dependent relationship with judgment, to relying on our own power to judge, weigh and make decisions to direct ourselves.

This has become an operating system which is actively dedicated to us living as "well" as possible *separated from God.* In this condition, we have to trust in our ability to direct ourselves, making us reliant on ourselves as the functioning god. Our ability to practically trust God either fades further away or is never established. The operating system, of reviewing, judging, and directing without God, is itself a barrier that teaches us, moment by moment, to trust ourselves, as it quietly locks us away from God.

> *Judgment convinces us that we are doing the correct thing because it makes us feel like all the resources of humankind are available to us to help make our decisions.*

Godhead of Self

The system is hard to see because judgment is the most compelling way to navigate life without God; if we do it, we believe in the practice. In using judgment, we are kept from God in a way that reinforces a perception that He is neither available nor kind. Judgment flatters us because we become the active godhead. It convinces us that we are doing the correct thing because it makes us feel like all the resources of humankind are available to us to help make our decisions. The Operating System of Judgment even makes the history of God on earth available for us to consider, study, and assess as the **godhead of ourselves** chooses the way forward that **we** most believe in. The Operating System of Judgment seems like a comprehensive navigational package. It can take us as far as considering and studying God and dedicating all our effort to Him as we (and our power to judge) direct our way.

Because the Operating System of Judgment has been our dominant civilizational operating system, shaping our ways of perceiving and the generational transmission of understanding, many have believed that guiding ourselves well into our idea of a godly lifestyle is being in relationship with God. Doing that, however, is both the product and the cause of God not being near. Traditionally, people are obsessed with Eve's disobedience. Usually the impact of her failure to comply with God's instruction is used to inspire us to do the right thing. But which right thing? And when? How? To work out those questions, most believers inadvertently turn harder into the Operating System of Judgment, the operating system that prospers disconnection.

The setting of the Garden of Eden positioned Adam and Eve close to all of God's goodness, in a "yada" relationship with Him, and with no direct experience of the power of evil. The word "yada" is used throughout Scripture for our relationship with God. In "yada," all of God is available to us and nothing in us is hidden from Him. Adam and Eve's knowledge of evil was gained through direct experience after they were tricked by the serpent. They were tricked away from a simple connection to God into an ecosystem that comprised the complex set of relational and governmental interactions that most people know as normal life. This is, in fact, the reality of a "yada" relationship with good and evil; it's what the devil promised Eve she would have. The fact that the operational change was represented in the Garden of Eden as a "tree" shows us that they were engaging with something that was a whole-of-life system. It had a deep foundation into the physical world (roots), a structure (branches), it created habitation, and it had an interaction with the spirit realm (leaves transpiring).

God never wanted Adam and Eve, nor anyone alive today, to have to navigate the intense and conflicted spiritual space created by the Operating System of Judgment - a legacy of the Tree of the Knowledge of Good and Evil. Adam and Eve were designed to live with God in a simple way of life that would always preserve them (and us) as part of His divine family. But Adam and Eve became weighed down with the heavy burden of an operating system that separated them from God. Understanding that there was an operating system change, gives us the freedom not to need an opinion about Adam and Eve's nature. The important thing to know is that, as long as we stay trapped in the Operating System of Judgment, we live out a life separated from the "nature" of God as Adam and Eve now were.

If we live according to the Operating System of Jesus, our life becomes increasingly an expression of God's nature. We are what God says we are: made in His image and "very good." The powers of evil that exist across all aspects of life on this planet have set their very best schemes against that expression of God's nature and the possibility that we too are intrinsically designed to be an expression of that goodness. Evil does whatever it can, including teaching us to judge and label our "nature," to entangle us and obscure our access to God.

Misplaced Faith

Outside of closeness to God, the spiritual environment of life on earth is so scary and confronting to the human spirit that people feel compelled to grab the closest God-like thing they can, usually the one they trust the most. This is almost universally a person's own self. The self, with its ability to think and feel, is clearly like God (made in His image), available, and reliably concerned with one's own best interest. The self is, therefore, the normal resource people lock onto to deal with the immense pressure of having to navigate through human life.

> *When Eve turned her mind into a tool of judgment, she was able to believe the otherwise unbelievable idea that she was better off guiding herself than trusting God.*

This putting faith in our own judgments, assumptions, emotions, and decision-making happens as quickly for us as it did for Eve. It leaves us unable to live out God's purposes for our lives and vulnerable to all kinds of harm; it carries with it the illusion of safety. It feels very much like operating in our Godlike dominion. It is a convincing replica of the life in God that we were born for, but the sure foundation of connection to God is not there.

When Eve turned her mind into a tool of judgment, she was able to believe the otherwise unbelievable idea that she was better off guiding herself than trusting God. Her decisions based on her own judgments became the only map for her life, what she could have and do, and how she would live. Adam and Eve became responsible to use whatever power and resources they could to take care of themselves. They became the determiners of their own destinies and, in doing so, acted out their Godlikeness without God. Once activated, there was no undoing that operating system. That would not be possible until God made a way back to connection with Himself through Jesus.

Without access to God, their human limits would define the outcomes of everything despite their intentions to do good. In this state, cut off from God, the source of good, mankind could not be allowed to live the way of eternity by eating from the Tree of Life. They had to leave the Garden of Eden to remove their access to it.

Despite the fact that it has now been 2000 years since mankind and the planet were given a revelation of Jesus, most believers persist in using an operating system that people were compelled to use when access to God was closed off. This is the deception and corruption referred to in 2 Corinthians 11:3. *"... lest somehow, as the serpent deceived Eve by his craftiness, so your minds may be corrupted from the simplicity that is in Christ."* Most of us are unaware that the operating system that Eve activated is still our default option. Until we choose to move into the operating system Jesus made available for us, we are, by default, under an operating system that limits our access to God. This was not what we were supposed to accept.

> *Without access to God, their human limits would define the outcomes of everything despite their intentions to do good.*

Here is the process that Eve activated and that millions of people keep alive today:

(1) Doubt God's kindness and good intentions.
(2) Trust our own judgment / assumptions about a situation.
(3) Decide on a course of action based on our own judgment.
(4) Inhabit the space of separation from God in which it is far more difficult for us to connect to Him than He intended.
(5) Compound the disconnection by making more guiding judgments out of that state of isolation from God.

Invitation

Jesus warned us repeatedly against judgment, but He was not just warning us not to say unkind words about people or advising us about Judgment Day. He was also warning us away from using judgment the way Eve did, as a power that directs an operating system keeping humanity locked away from Him. He was inviting us back into childlike trust. Let's have a look at what Jesus had to say about judgment.

"Judgment" in Greek is the word "krino." It translates to mean a separating, an accusing, a slandering, or a forming of an opinion or a decision. In "krino," we are separated from God, by ourselves, so our decisions are directed by assessing, reviewing, measuring, analyzing, and "working out" what is "best," "right," or "Godly," rather than being directed through a connection to God. Krino actually removes us from our union with God and brings the destructive state of separation from Him right into the core of life.

Jesus told us that judgment causes us to be sent away to "the accuser," "the council," (the Jewish Sanhedrin) and "jail" (Matthew 5:25), and leads us on the path towards the eternal fire (Matthew 10:28). Corporately, the outworking of this includes: division, disunity, separation, competition, control, suspicion, and hard work protecting the interests of our "group." Individually, the effects of the Operating System of Judgment are even more painful - a vast range of destructive effects throughout generations and in every family line.

Perhaps most destructive of all of the effects on the individual is the splitting of self that Jesus often referred to when He called the Pharisees "hypocrites." The word Jesus used is derived from "hypokrinomai" which means either to play a part on a stage as an actor, or to answer to an accusation or suggestion and to decide for oneself in relation to that allegation or suggestion. The root of the word krino or "judge" is in there, but the prefix "hypo" describes a process of someone doing judgment reflexively, or back on oneself.

> *A person who navigates by judgment comes into a relationship with the accuser and has to act out their life in response to the torment caused by that constant stream of accusation.*

In short, a person who navigates by judgment comes into a relationship with the accuser and has to act out their life in response to the torment caused by that constant stream of accusation. The term "hypocrite" does not refer to a person who is saying one thing and doing something else. Jesus is describing "hypocrites" as different entities. They are split beings with a vicious internal dialogue that makes it impossible for them to live well, let alone to represent God. "*Woe to you, scribes and Pharisees, hypocrites! For you travel land and sea to win one proselyte (convert), and when he is won, you make him twice as much a son of hell as yourselves*" (Matthew 23:15).

A hypocrite is not a whole person living in direct connection to God. A hypocrite is a person acting out what they perceive to be the right/best/correct response to the allegation, accusation, and slander that is happening inside their own spirit. Their life has become dedicated to playing out the "right" part in a civilization that is a construct, like a film set built by the power of judgment to keep them out of the much larger and much more compelling realities that God has for them. Jesus' life was a clear display of a new reality of union to God; a clear break from the imprisoning realities created by the Pharisees, a faith community who were devoted to God but lived under the Operating System of Judgment.

In John 16:8 Jesus tells of the Holy Spirit, "And when He has come, He will convict the world of sin, and of righteousness, and of **judgment.**" Jesus came to release the planet from the inheritance of the Tree of the Knowledge of Good and Evil, the Operating System of Judgment. The false god in that system is our own ability to judge and form opinions in our minds. Functioning according to "beliefs" that we "decide" to be "the best" or "correct," as opposed to living in connection to God (doing and saying what He has for us to do), will not give us the abundant life in God that Jesus said He came to bring (John 10:10b). It will trap us, divide us, separate us, limit us, and make us the victims of what we do not understand. Contrast that with the life of union with God (the "Tree of Life") where we know that we are on His pathway, we prosper out of our union with Him, and we see His purposes come to pass through our lives, delivering the God who is beyond all that we can think or imagine to situations where He is what is desperately needed. Jesus bought back for us the opportunity to live in the operating system that Eve unknowingly gave away.

> *A hypocrite is not a whole person living in direct connection to God.*

Sin, Judgment, and Righteousness

Jesus came to convict the world of **sin** and **righteousness** and **judgment** (John 16:8). There were three people crucified on the day Jesus was executed. On those crosses that day **righteousness** prevailed. Jesus' righteous death became the way to resurrection life, and the power of **sin** and **judgment** were terminated. One criminal got free from the power of sin and

36

was told by Jesus that they would be together in Paradise (Luke 23:43). On Jesus' other side, the criminal stayed locked in judgment all the way to death, declaring his doubt, assumptions, and judgment: *"If you are the Christ, save yourself and save us"* (Luke 23:39).

This criminal was bound by the operating system into a way of seeing. From inside that perspective, what Jesus was doing was of no use. That day the power of **sin** and **judgment** were broken and God's **righteousness** was made available for all people for the rest of time. Despite Jesus making a pathway back to unimpeded access to God, the Operating System of Judgment can still be used to reinstate the deadly separation.

Any time we **direct** our lives in response to *our* judgment, assumption, assessment, consideration, or weighing of options, we operate in our godlikeness without God, and begin to live away from intimate union with Him and towards captivity and demonic oppression. Many people are led down this road, believing that God wants them to guide themselves "biblically" in His name, and that their own innate ability to judge, direct, and make assessments (their God-likeness) will steer them through that journey. It is the same corruption of the mind that caused Adam and Eve to hide from God after they disobeyed Him.

> *Any time we direct our lives in response to our judgment, we operate in our godlikeness without God.*

It is the Operating System of Judgment, this way of functioning, that reduces our access to God and raises people who have beliefs *about* God rather than people who have *Him*. With the best intentions, people set out to raise "godly" children, or disciple new converts into what they have decided is necessary to know about living a Christian life. Unwittingly, they offer the very choice that Eve was offered in the Garden of Eden. Put aside the particulars of the actual beliefs and think about this: Children and new believers are presented with this option: "Believe this package of beliefs, decide that you will guide yourself by them, and you will be in relationship with God."

Unfortunately, this actually activates people into their own godlikeness under the Operating System of Judgment. A person becomes sold on the value of their beliefs and on faith in their own ability to judge. They enter into an imprisoning operating system, when their deepest desire is to know God. There now exists a barrier between them and God. It is very sad for people to live in the reality of this barrier when in their hearts they genuinely wanted to place their lives into God's hands.

Mike's Story

Mike was concerned because his daughter wanted to start dating a guy who had apparently only been a Christian for a few months. "Ideally," he said, "she would take a year or two while this guy becomes a more mature Christian." Mike shared his concerns, describing what he wanted for his daughter.

I asked Mike how his story of meeting his spouse and dating went. He reflected, "We did really know very, very deeply that God had brought us together." He realized the opportunity he had to let the next generation build their marriages as he had, out of a deep knowing from God, rather than a human assessment of what constitutes "Christian maturity" or "godly wisdom."

Spiritual Transactions

Belief in the value of making judgments is the start of a spiritual transaction that pulls us away from God. It is the same spiritual transaction that tricked Eve. In practice, the Operating System of Judgment leaves people vulnerable to condemnation and insecurity. When we choose to operate out of judgment, it is instated as a spiritual power and the devil has legal right to harass us, judge us, or pressure us to judge ourselves.

Arming ourselves with beliefs that counteract the denigration will never terminate the vulnerability, neither will strategies or goals that we devise out of our own ability to judge. As long as we are operating from our finite mind, the tormenting spirits will see the exact details of the spiritual lockdown that we inhabit while we remain blind to their existence. They can harass, undermine, and restrict us from the other side of our limitations. We will be exhausted before they run out of strategies.

Not everyone inside the captivity of the Operating System of Judgment feels tormented. If a person is prepared to act as an agent of the operating system *(for example discipling people into a judgment-based culture)* then the pressure may shift, but the only permanent solution to torment is to become a person whose life is founded in God and who operates the same way Jesus did. Aside from God Himself, a person who "knows" God is the most powerful creature in the whole spirit realm. In John 15, we are encouraged to "abide" (fully live) in the vine. Psalm 91:1 describes what that is like. It tells us about the person who "abides" in God. The Psalm concludes by declaring that all the protection and resources named are available because the person "knows" God's name. The word is "yada," intimate union. Jesus died for us to have this intimate union.

Psalm 91

1. He who dwells in the secret place of the Most High
   Shall abide under the shadow of the Almighty.
2. I will say of the Lord, "He is my refuge and my fortress;
   My God, in Him I will trust."
3. Surely He shall deliver you from the snare of the fowler[a]
   And from the perilous pestilence.
4. He shall cover you with His feathers,
   And under His wings you shall take refuge;
   His truth shall be your shield and buckler.
5. You shall not be afraid of the terror by night,
   Nor of the arrow that flies by day,
6. Nor of the pestilence that walks in darkness,
   Nor of the destruction that lays waste at noonday.
7. A thousand may fall at your side,
   And ten thousand at your right hand;
   But it shall not come near you.
8. Only with your eyes shall you look,
   And see the reward of the wicked.
9. Because you have made the Lord, who is my refuge,
   Even the Most High, your dwelling place,
10. No evil shall befall you,
    Nor shall any plague come near your dwelling;
11. For He shall give His angels charge over you,
    To keep you in all your ways.
12. In their hands they shall bear you up,
    Lest you dash your foot against a stone.
13. You shall tread upon the lion and the cobra,
    The young lion and the serpent you shall trample underfoot.
14. Because he has set his love upon Me, therefore I will deliver him;
    I will set him on high, because he has known My name.
15. He shall call upon Me, and I will answer him;
    I will be with him in trouble;
    I will deliver him and honor him.
16. With long life I will satisfy him,
    And show him My salvation."

Childlikeness

Only being a son or daughter of God, positioned and resourced by Him because our life has become a part of His purposes, will position us in a strength that intimidates the powers of darkness. The spirit realm has always known that the safest and most opportunity-rich way for a person to live is grafted into intimate union with God. For that reason, evil keeps up a dedicated onslaught against the discovery of the childlike simplicity of knowing God. It will keep us driving forward. We will be looking for a goal, an aim, and a purpose that we can pursue "in God's name," pushing us with every possible strategy into "yada" with good and evil and away from "yada" with God.

The Operating System of Judgment skews peoples' reading of history and makes it easy for evil to twist all of our perceptions. It can be very hard to walk out of perceptions that we believed were truths and walk into an operating system that keeps everything open and free. Eve was the first person to start to narrow down her options to what she believed in the moment that she could trust.

> *For that reason, evil keeps up a dedicated onslaught against the discovery of the childlike simplicity of knowing God.*

God was desperately saddened by the consequences and paid everything for us to have a way back to the connection with Him. God knew that it would be impossible for people who had lived into a corrupted way of thinking to think their way out of the corruption. A person who has become trained into a corrupt way of seeing is very difficult to re-wire. Anything that gets communicated into the jail gets distorted by the prison guards. They edit and twist our hearing of God's inputs.

As a consequence, our communication back to God is also distorted. It is corrupted by our misperceptions of Him. We request things of Him in prayer that would drive us further into the operating system that harms us if God gave us what we asked for. Our inability to perceive what God is doing prevents us from praying in alignment with His purposes. Communication between God and man and man and God is muffled and distorted by the separation caused by the Operating System of Judgment.

When God wanted to put safeguards around a population living in a corrupt system, He sent very clear instructions carved in stone (the Ten Commandments). But to uncorrupt the operating system of people on the earth and set us free to be one with Him, He needed to send something deeply compelling. He needed to send something incorruptible (Himself) and in a way that is real and evident, something tangible and exactly how God wanted it to be rather than a written or spoken message that could be edited by the "officers of the jail" and the "prison guards." God knew if He sent a demonstration (Jesus) and made a way that He Himself could become our guide (Holy Spirit), then He could reconnect to us and walk with us back into the certainty of relationship with Him.

Chapter 3

OUR GODLIKENESS – WITH GOD OR WITHOUT HIM?

Genesis 1:26 *"Then God said, "Let Us make man in Our image, according to Our likeness; let them have dominion..."*

We know that God was pleased with His creation and called it "good;" we also know that He intended for His children to have dominion. In the Garden of Eden, God created humans to be genuinely like Him. Like Him they had (and we still have) the ability to exercise dominion. This differentiates us from all the other created beings. Whatever cannot exercise dominion is not Godlike in the sense that we are. A goldfish is not godlike. It is clearly God inspired and reflects His creative genius, but it cannot bring things under its own rulership and governance. The essence of human-God-likeness is that we are designed to operate as governmental agents undoing the government of the powers of darkness and replacing it with God's government which is love and life. God's dominion is a dominion of love and life, displacing hatred and death. If we are connected to Him, the power that flows through us displaces realities that have less life or less love.

> *Whatever cannot exercise dominion is not Godlike in the sense that we are.*

We are created to join our potential as Godlike beings to God. This is us, fully available, to be an extension of His nature, and in doing so, God is delivered through us in the precise measure necessary to complete any task He has for us to do. All of creation is crying out for this. We were meant to know this. We were meant to understand it and enjoy the perfection of how His system works for us. Human beings are not designed to live disconnected from the power of God. The living power of God that radically overturns dark circumstances for good is supposed to be in our frame of reference.

We are wired to know what life feels like when God gets to be God through us. People were designed to experience the intense power of God moving through their bodies to cause healing. We are supposed to have the experience of praying words that come directly from God to quash anxiety, doubt, and fear in even the most frightening situations. God meant us to know, for example, that irreconcilable differences in marriages will be reconciled when we pray. We are built to respond to such assignments out of a primal knowing that our prayer is required and redemption wins.

The Kingdom of God is a network of people joined together in righteous love, through which the power of God is free to flow so that whatever God chooses can happen. It makes all of us a united extension of Him (John 17). The experience of God's perfect administration of power through us for His purposes is a compelling reason for submitting all of our Godlike potential to God's direct government and His real divinity.

> *Human beings are not designed to live disconnected from the power of God. The living power of God that radically overturns dark circumstances for good is supposed to be in our frame of reference. We are wired to know what life feels like when God gets to be God through us.*

Wiring for God-Likeness

When people become separated from God and held away from Him by the Operating System of Judgment, their intrinsic God-given need for relationship with power, and for an expression of dominion still exists. The relationship with power instead becomes very much devoted to harnessing whatever resources and talents are available to an individual to make their own way prosper, and as much as possible, to protect their interests from harm. The hard-wiring towards dominion is displaced sideways onto interpersonal relationships and causes competition, rivalry, and any form of the assumption that one person must displace another for the one to succeed. This is displayed in the strife between Cain and Abel as the first generation born under the Operating System of Judgment.

At the beginning of human history, Adam and Eve had the same choice we do; to fulfill their God-like potential by living into union with God or to live out of their God-like abilities as best they can without Him. They got to make the choice for generations of people after them. They could have immediately started multiplying, naming animals, taking dominion, and enacting their Godlikeness out of the intimate access to God already built into His design.

> *Adam and Eve were set up for success, for "normal life" in God but chose faith in themselves instead.*

Adam and Eve were set up for success, for "normal life" in God but chose faith in themselves instead. Thanks to Jesus making a way for us to be reconnected to Father God, we have the option of normal life being a life lived with God. God has determined that this option will always be available. How is it that billions have been tricked into trying to live out their godlike potential without Him?

So the two options for how we live into our god-like potential are:

1. **Fulfilling our God-likeness in union with God:** We connect to God as our Father, and allow His divinity to pour into us through that connection. As we subjugate our godlikeness to His real Godness, our godlikeness is fulfilled through union with His divine nature and power; His love flowing through us displaces darkness. We become people of His dominion. The living reality of God presents itself through us to the people and the world around us. God displays Himself through us as He is, life streaming into places that had been entangled with death.

2. **Fulfilling our God-likeness directed by our own power to judge (a false godhead):**
   In this mode, we enact our godlikeness without connection to God. Rather than letting our personhood become intertwined with His divinity, we remain in-charge of our own thinking and decision-making. All our acts of dominion are governed by our own mind, which makes our decisions based on our reflections about right and wrong, risk versus reward, strengths versus vulnerabilities, opportunities versus fears, and on what we think we know.

   In this system, the active working of God through people is absent. Operating as an agent of judgment directly defies God the Father's desires for people and defies what Jesus did on the cross. It sets limits on God, and leaves people vulnerable to schemes authored by the demonic realm.

The devil told Eve that the Tree of the Knowledge of Good and Evil would make her "see like God" (Gen 3). He was not lying, but omitted that she would be seeing similarly to Him, but without Him. Having forsaken the option of living in intimate union with Him ("yada" knowing), she gave up the option to see what He is seeing, move when He does, speak what He wants spoken, and do what He wants done in His world in His perfect timing. Instead, the best available earthly life under this operating system is limited to the natural laws and wise principles that undergird all of creation. In deciding on this option, we have chosen to be able to "see *like* God" rather than "see *from* God."

So our seeing and knowing is diminished, but our belief in our efforts to govern ourselves is immense. We humans have a subconscious awe of our ability to make independent decisions based on our own judgments. We become so seduced by this ability that it actually lands us in a prison of our own making. As our eyes and minds become falsely "enlightened" to the judgment of earthly things, our ability to see what is going on in the heavenly realms of God is vastly diminished. Thankfully, the converse is also true, that when we are with God looking at the paths of life that He is creating, our ability to see what evil is trying to achieve will also be increased. Anything that reduces our connection is forced to disclose its own nature when we become people who only operate out of our connection to God.

God's Network of Power

People living out their godlikeness without God, under the Operating System of Judgment, create and inhabit territory that is essentially "off limits" to God. In that territory, they are extremely vulnerable to any scheme of hell directed their way. God will usually allow people to reap the fruit of whatever evil structures they have authorized. He doesn't want it for us, but He is faithful to Himself and to the freedom He created for us. His nature compels Him to offer us the freedom to choose to govern ourselves, but the outcome is not His heart for us. If we choose self-governance, He will never stop wooing us into an altogether safer place.

Even when we lock ourselves down in a way that makes it almost impossible for us to sense Him, He is never far away. His deepest desire is to *"draw all men unto [Himself]"* (John 12:32), but a human who has given themselves accidentally to the service of the judge in their own mind, may keep propelling themselves away from the God who is calling them to Himself.

Jesus has made it possible to restore the connection between God and mankind that God always wanted. God's original idea was to have an intimate relationship with children made in His image - godlike and free. His nature longs for relationship, but our freedom of choice left open a pathway to separation from God. That separation is so radically unacceptable to God that He paid a very high price to provide us with a way to come into close connection. Jesus is the restoration plan. For God's redemptive purpose, Jesus adopted the form of a human, and yielded His divine attributes completely to the will of the Father.

Jesus was required by the Father to live a human life, through which the divine nature that they had in common was displayed, precisely in alignment with the Father's will. It was this commitment to the will of the Father that made Jesus' life a demonstration of the Father's dominion, beginning the Kingdom of God on the earth. In the same way that Jesus submitted His divinity to The Father we are invited to submit our godlikeness to the Father. We become agents of His dominion. As we do, the Kingdom of God advances through us.

Followers of Jesus in the early centuries of Christianity were called, "*Followers of the Way*" (Acts 9:2). When people today long for the explosive transformation that early believers witnessed, they seldom realize they are longing to be a people who did not have access to an instruction manual. Those first followers did not have a book. It was much harder for them to keep their faith as a cognitive exercise. They had to find the living God. After Holy Spirit came, they like Jesus, did and said what God was doing and saying. They followed The **Truth**, Jesus, who came alive to them and became their **way** to experience the resurrection **life** of God the Father (John 14:6).

The devil will do anything to keep us from offering ourselves into God's network of power, His dominion. Evil still uses the strategy of prompting us to consult our own minds to find "*our* way" forward. But when we get close to the one who made us and then declared that everything He made was good, we can eat of the Tree of Life and live out His divine nature through our union with Father God. We become the eternal-life sons and daughters who respond to Him by choosing an open connection to all the aspects of His infinite nature and power. His dominion will advance throughout all of life and all regions of the planet. People will get to experience God as He is.

Setting the Scene for Redemption

After thousands of years under the Operating System of Judgment, civilization was well acquainted with the problems caused by humans exercising godlike dominion. By the time of the Pharisees, the Jewish people had one of the most highly refined cultures ever to be crafted out of the Operating System of Judgment. Every single moment of Jewish life was structured by a rule, and all of those rules came out of some thoughtfully-considered judgment of how to be righteous. The Pharisees were devoted, loyal, God-fearing people who wanted to take care of orphans and widows and spend their lives doing good in the name of God, but their operating system was inherited from the Tree of the Knowledge of Good and Evil. Because of this, it was a life-sucking, burdensome system.

It was into this pharisaic culture of the Operating System of Judgment that John the Baptist was sent. He prophesied the end of the legacy of the Tree of the Knowledge of Good and Evil and the reconnection of mankind to God through Jesus. He declared, "*The axe has already been put to the root of the tree*" (Matthew 3:10). Jesus came into that oppressive culture to offer life under an "*easy yoke*" (Matthew 11:30). His burden would be light. He offered the opportunity to be reborn into His family as children of a loving Father God and live a life of total trust, directed by *Him*.

It was in the original position of total trust with God that the devil found us. He tricked us away from God with a suggestion that he had information about God that we didn't and convinced us that our lack of knowing would hurt us.

After judging God and activating themselves as agents of the Operating System of Judgment, people fell into judgments of one another. In fact, inside the Operating System of Judgment, all relationships are judgment oriented and directed. Inside the limited realities of the Operating System of Judgment, people are not functioning as they are meant to. They are not functioning as a living conduit of God- an extension of God Himself. The disconnection from God is a disconnection from the source of truth. Any assessment made in that condition will not be true. It can, in some way, refer to truth, but it cannot be the fullness of truth.

The Operating System of Judgment alleges that from Adam and Eve on, the nature of people, their very essence, became sinful. Furthermore, it tells us that God rejected Adam and

Eve, and cursed them out of the Garden of Eden as punishment for their disobedience and for failing His test. But those are not the words used nor concepts described in God's account of the story. God told Adam and Eve how life would be under the system they had activated, the Operating System of Judgment.

Everything that God described about Adam and Eve's future after they were to leave the Garden of Eden and outside of close connection to Him were natural consequences, the essential marking of jurisdictional boundaries, and the hierarchical power structures that must exist in a governmental system that is separate from God. In that governmental system, every moment of pain, every limitation, and every relational tension advertises the nature of the government in the system. Each moment of pain is an opportunity for a person to look for the better option. It is an invitation back into the relationship with God and out of the burden of self-government. All of the tensions and inadequacies are inbuilt markers of the heavy burden being carried unnecessarily by the population, a reminder of the lack of divine direction and empowerment.

> *In His kindness, God began to tend mankind towards His goal of complete redemption.*

Unable to access God, Adam and Eve would wear the full brunt of the forces of the natural world, guided by their own best intentions in reference to their own intrinsic God-likeness. God sent Adam and Eve out of the Garden of Eden, away from their access to the Tree of Life, so that the corruption would not last forever. If they had stayed and eaten from the Tree of Life they would have actually lived forever (eternal life) but under their own direction, not God's. God did not want that outcome. It was not His nature to empower eternal conflict. In His kindness, God began to tend mankind towards His goal of complete redemption.

Battlefield of Judgment

Although thousands of years have passed since Jesus Christ demonstrated a way that was so clearly desirable, we are tempted into the pressures and constraints of an illegal and illegitimate battle by endless claims and allegations created by the Operating System of Judgment. People of every nation are bound by a great weight of inherited cultural entanglements to fight out the merits of one or another set of ideas.

As long as humans live out their aspirations in the warzone created and carefully protected by the Operating System of Judgment, the "freedom" that God has secured and made available to everyone will be falsely presented by well-meaning believers in forms that are little more than constantly evolving or alternating patterns of demands and constrictions. Sooner or later people find out that they have given their hearts to another set of judgment-derived behaviors and cultural demands. The disappointment is a cause of very real pain, the long-lasting scars of a battle that should be over.

The energy of the battleground is easily maintained. One group of people rationally assign themselves a label based on any particular set of shared behaviors. They rally around any judgment or assumptions of a different group, Christians for instance, that is not consistent with their own, and a battle line is drawn.

Take the assertion that non-traditional marriages should be made legal. These assertions are thrown into the ring so that the people who purport to represent God can be triggered into making responses. The Pharisees were always trying to entangle Jesus. Jesus came back with "live" ammunition from a different economy; an economy that opens up love and life with every interaction. People in the Operating System of Judgment do it differently. Here, the operative in the system has to **work out** how to display "Godly" love, or how to appropriately or realistically live out a demonstration of "biblical values" in such a supposedly "complex" social context.

The classification and labeling of people according to their behaviors, a reality in the Operating System of Judgment, does not exist in the Kingdom of God. In the Old Testament, God demonstrated to us that His nature and way did not generate choices the same way people did without Him. God's choices to raise up David and Joseph made that point. Both were considered less impressive than their older brothers. The Operating System of Judgment would have deemed a different person to be more suited to the future job descriptions of these two men.

Similarly, when Jesus chose His disciples, He did not choose them because of any distinguishing giftings. We are not told that there was any "qualifying" process at all. Occasionally, a person in the stories of Jesus is given a label, usually one with a negative connotation. We are told that Zacchaeus was a "tax collector" but Jesus did not call him that, nor did Jesus even address the "issue" of the man's ill-gotten wealth. Apparently, Zacchaeus just reformed himself because Jesus was with him (Luke 19).

In the Kingdom of God, everyone has an invitation to complete access to God. On our individual journey, we all have the option to live out our own complete union with Him. Past behaviors, desires, misunderstandings, offenses, and victories do not create realities for God, nor for us. Paul described this radical change when he said, "There is neither Jew nor Greek, there is neither slave nor free, there is neither male nor female;

for you are all one in Christ Jesus" (Galatians 3:28). Jesus is the redeemer of all things and knows exactly how to be the light that interrupts someone's journey, pulling them out of darkness that might otherwise be so compelling when access to Him is barred.

Our inability to operate in the infinite power of God has coerced us into remaining practitioners of the Operating System of Judgment, forcing us to be happy with the fact that a sin-labeled group might appreciate it when we stem the flow of our moral correction to a trickle, divert it onto a different group, or turn it back on ourselves. All the while, groups of believers are creating strategy in a war cabinet established by the devil himself on a battlefield of the Operating System of Judgment; everyone on the battlefield is a volunteer, giving their life for a war that was not commissioned by God. If we let the Operating System of Judgment tell us what battles to fight, then the limitations of humanity will tell history why it would have been better if we had done things differently.

People are slow to let go of the excitement of the battle because the adrenaline and sense of purpose are a substitute for the real experience of God's power. Instead of relationship with God, we stay connected to dark sets of beliefs about ourselves and then choose, in our own power, how to most appropriately live out some idea of what redemption should look like. This ensures that under the Operating System of Judgment God's followers become just the same as any other group of people that has formed a culture or a lifestyle out of the daily expression of their darkest fears about themselves. In that loveless place, God seems far away. It traps us deep within a system that takes all that we have and gives the world nothing like what we are hoping to get - The clear display of God and the invitation to Him that we would want to be the result of our life and love poured out.

Pulling Away

We must pull away from the toxic fabrication that the powers of evil work so hard to foist onto the people of this planet. Whether we are inside of church being asked to believe we are a sinner, a saint who was a sinner, or outside of church being taught to believe that our desires generate our behaviors and our behaviors dictate our "identity," we all have the opportunity to refuse to play by the code. Refusal to play by the code the jailers offer us will keep our senses free, opening up our environment to the reality of God and giving us back the space and time to connect with God as He is, so that He can teach us His ways. Understanding the elements that comprise the two operating systems helps us to allow God to train us out of one system and into His.

The Operating System of Jesus, The Legacy of the Tree of Life:

•Childlike knowledge of God's goodness with a perception of Him that matches the one at the time of creation. We know we were created by Him and that He approves of everything about His design of us.

•People learn to live from a deep union with God, ultimately living directly from His nature and ways.

•Ongoing access to transformational power and unquenchable love from God.

•Intimacy with the Father. He knows us by name, always has us with Him, and is always delighted by the access He has to our hearts.

•Circumstances authored by God and not vulnerable to schemes authored by evil.

The Operating System of Judgment, The Legacy of the Tree of the Knowledge of Good and Evil:

•A perverted perception of God. Love, kindness, and goodness are not dominant descriptions of a person's experience with Him. God looks stern, rigid, and disapproving.

•Very limited access to mercy. Mercy does not flow naturally through or between people who operate in judgment. Despite intellectual assent to the idea of God's mercy, the cultures created on the Operating System of Judgment focus on what is "wrong" or "right" with themselves and others. Scripture is clear that Jesus' dominant posture to this time in the history of planet earth is mercy. If people are not postured in mercy, they must have some other "justification" ("judgment-based deduction") to support their divergence from Him.

•Difficulty trusting God.

•Compliance with a code replaces obedience to God. The Operating System of Judgment separates well-intentioned people from God. Unable to hear from or know God, and, therefore, unable to do what He would like them to do, they are consigned to creating and complying with prescriptions and codes.

• People guided by ideas, beliefs, rules and principles (Christian or secular).

> *Refusal to play by the code the jailers offer us will keep our senses free, opening up our environment to the reality of God and giving us back the space and time to connect with God.*

Yvette's Story

Yvette introduced me to her brother. He was in his mid-thirties and in a wheelchair. He had cerebral palsy and he couldn't speak or walk. I asked God how to pray and what to do. I felt to say, "Caleb, I think your Mom is going to get to hear you speak." Two weeks later, Yvette came up to me very enthusiastically. "Guess what! Caleb spoke for the first time ever. His first word was "Mom" and also "I love you" and about ten other words so far." A simple phrase, taken from what I felt God was saying, released healing over this man in a way they had never experienced.

Chapter 4

THE DESIRE FOR ONENESS

On the night that Jesus was going to be betrayed by Judas, leading to His crucifixion, He prepared Himself in a conversation with His Father, God. This next part of His journey would be searingly difficult. A detailed account of the moments just before the greatest ordeal of Jesus' earthly life is found in John 17. In this tender moment, Jesus prays not only for His disciples, but for all people who "pisteuo eis eme..." "trust themselves into me" (John 17:20-21). It goes on to say,

> *'I do not pray for these alone (Jesus disciples), but also for those who will believe in Me through their word (the disciples' testimony); that they all may be one, as You, Father, [are] in Me, and I in You; that they also may be one in Us that the world may believe that You sent Me.'*

John 17

About eight years ago, I had an encounter with God while reading John 17. At the time, I thought this chapter was all about Jesus' desire for church unity. It was preached to quiet down disruptive, rebellious, or crazy elements in the church. I presumed it to be the artillery used to silence any challenge to the status quo. This use of John 17 fuels the belief that Jesus wants us all to be polite, all in agreement, and well-behaved together. But, it is an example of Jesus, the Son of God, and I watched Him talking to His Dad. Only moments before being arrested, He prayed to His Father, and then walked over to the garden where He knew Judas would bring soldiers to take Him captive.

Jesus' longing was for ALL people who believe.

I was amazed that His words barely touched on His impending suffering but poured out concern for His disciples after He was put to death. Jesus loved these men and gave them everything He had. The disciples abandoned their previous lives and followed Jesus for years. Despite some ups and downs, they regarded Him as the Son of God, strongly depending on Him for many things. Simon Peter once asked, "*Lord, to whom shall we go? You have the words of eternal life*" (John 6:68). These men surrendered their whole selves to Jesus, and He greatly loved them.

The vulnerability of Jesus struck me profoundly as He discussed with His Father how it felt to leave His friends behind. He laid out a request to God. Jesus said He wanted His disciples and everyone who heard about Him through their testimony to live in intimate union with the Father and Himself. This was the very same intimacy Jesus and His Father held. As I read this, I was overcome. Jesus' grief at leaving the disciples was only bearable if they were going to be better off, if their separation did not indeed extend into the spirit realm. Thankfully, He was organizing for the opposite of separation, a complete union; they, we, would become inseparable and indistinguishable from God. He made a plea to the Father for structural union- complete oneness.

Did the Father grant Jesus' request? We know He did because we know Jesus' operating system. Jesus only did and said what He knew the Father was doing and saying. "*I say to you, the Son can do nothing of Himself, but what He sees the Father do; for whatever He does, the Son also does in like manner*" (John 5:19). "*In and of Myself, I can do nothing*" (John 5:30). If Jesus prayed it, we can be certain it was in the Father's heart for Him to pray it, so we know this record of Jesus asking for us to be one with God and Himself was also an indication of the Father's heart that we would all be one. The assumption that this chapter is merely a call to the Christian church to be united has blocked people from seeing the full implication of this prayer. Indeed, the fullness of what Jesus made possible must be apprehended.

Intimate Union

God's longing for union with people is intense. The powers of darkness would like us to believe that Him desiring us so intensely is somehow a breach of His holiness, but His desire for us is unending. We are perfectly made by God in the image of Himself. A heart of longing is a gift by design that propels us on the journey towards His heart. Longing for intimate union is both our nature and the nature of God.

Marriage is an enduring symbol of the innate human desire for permanent union to another. It is a universal cultural phenomenon. In western culture, people marry for love, hoping the marriage will prosper as an expression of love. Because love is God and God is love, our ability to love comes from Him, so the way to navigate anything as an expression of love through time is the Operating System of Jesus. Intimate union with God gives Him the opportunity to make all of His capacity available to us. That is the infinite power of love. If we navigate by the Operating System of Judgment, dynamics that undermine the expression of love and make marriage very complex, become unavoidable. These judgment-based dynamics are the source of much of the undermining of marriage.

> *Intimate union with God gives Him the opportunity to make all of His capacity available to us.*

Two people who both navigate life using the Operating System of Judgment represent two separate governmental entities. Much hard work and negotiation may be required for a marriage comprising two such entities to survive. The complexity is akin to the difficulty of combining two political parties to achieve the governing of a nation, trusting a foreign government to gather our nation's intelligence, or agreeing to trust someone else's immune system to protect our own.

The Operating System of Judgment appoints self to the role of godhead and the self bears full responsibility for the protection and success of the individual. Self-interest is a prerequisite to survival in the Operating System of Judgment. This hard wiring pushes marriage towards being a legal arrangement; in this scenario, the best outcome that can be expected is mutual benefit.

When God is allowed to carry the weight of being the functioning Godhead, He is ultimately responsible for the protection and success of the people and a marriage union. He is much better qualified and resourced to ensure that the joining of two into one new governmental entity will create more than the sum of both people. Two individuals united under God are free to inhabit the posture of peace, fully connected to God's infinite strength. The instincts towards self-preservation that are strong influences in the Operating System of Judgment are replaced by the confidence that comes with access to God's infinite wisdom and ability; as a result, people become very safe. It is a multidimensional uniting of two people and God, a cord of three strands that is not easily broken (Ecclesiastes 4:12b).

When union under God occurs, the marriage becomes an unhindered expression of God. There are now no governmental barriers between the husband and wife and between God or both of them and God. In the Operating

System of Judgment, those separate governments would remain as barriers to the free flow of God through the marriage. In an attempt to force such a situation to represent God in the way that we believe it should, we would have to prescribe the behaviors we reasonably believe would most likely create the effect we judge to be most valuable. This results in a contrived imitation of an actual union.

Vulnerability

The benefit of living into the mutual "vulnerability" of marriage is that we get unimpeded access to God's strength. Rather than being a commitment to a complex legal agreement, marriage becomes a tender resting place for the infinite power of God. Marriage becomes an earthly representation of the fulfillment, multiplicity, and unity, three beings (wife, husband, and God) functioning as one organism creating unlimited love and life - an earthly manifestation of the triune God, the God who is three and one.

Even under the Operating System of Judgment and its pressure towards self-interest, our greatest desire is still for union. We long, as Jesus did, for full relational completion. Our spirits recognize that all of history is building towards a wedding. And we, the people of planet earth are the longed-for bride; God's gift to Himself, and His honoring of the work of Jesus. God shares our need for marriage as an expression of what is in our nature. Our desire for marriage comes from God.

> *The benefit of living into the mutual "vulnerability" of marriage is that we get unimpeded access to God's strength.*

In Jeremiah 33:11, the prophet describes the sound of the Bride's voice at the end of time. He records the following:

> "The voice of joy and the voice of gladness, the voice of the bridegroom and the voice of the bride, the voice of those who will say:
> "Praise the LORD of hosts,
> For the LORD *is* good,
> For His mercy *endures* forever"—
> *and* of those *who will* bring the sacrifice of praise into the house of the LORD. For I will cause the captives of the land to return **as at the first**,' says the LORD."

The Bride knows that God is good, that He operates in mercy rather than judgment, and that He returns the spiritual captives of the earth to the way people were supposed to be "as at first," peacefully walking in a garden in intimate union with God, their friend. Intimacy is the personal preference of God, and He has demonstrated that all of history is building towards a corporate oneness; His Bride.

Chapter 5

JESUS DEFEATED JUDGMENT

In John 5:24, Jesus says, *"Most assuredly, I say to you, he who hears My word and believes in Him who sent Me has everlasting life, and shall not come into judgment, but has passed from death into life."* Jesus regularly provides this contrast between the way of judgment that leads to death, and the invitation to give our lives into Him and live into the way of eternal life.

Both the teaching of Jesus and the life lived out by Him are examples that open up this profoundly different *"way."* The prophets foretold the Kingdom of God would come to the world with a great shift in the legal condition on the earth (Daniel 7:22). It would be a shift from judgment into mercy. A shift that would make it possible for us to live connected to God and experience the eternal fruit of that connection in an earthly setting and into eternity. What the prophets foretold, Jesus came to teach and demonstrate. He is the Tree of Life and we are *"the New Jerusalem,"* God's city built up around that tree (Rev 22:2).

Jesus devoted years of His life to presenting His living truth to people so that we could connect with His invitation into the way of life. In Luke 12, Jesus delivers one of the most powerful teachings on the opportunity. He urges people to let go of earthly cares and concerns and, instead, be established in eternal relationship with His Father. He promises us that, if we do, we will be better off, even better cared for, than Solomon himself.

In Luke 12:29-30, Jesus tenderly addresses the human predisposition to anxiety and fear, telling us, *"And do not seek what you should eat or what you should drink, nor have an anxious*

> *Jesus partners His tenderness with absolute conviction that He is inviting us into a better way.*

mind." He goes on to reassure us, *"For all these things the nations of the world seek after, and your Father knows that you need these things."* He clearly states that choosing to pursue one thing in particular, the Kingdom of God, will open up every other possibility *"But seek the kingdom of God, and all these things shall be added to you"* (Luke 12:31). Jesus partners His tenderness with absolute conviction that He is inviting us into a better way, a more powerful reality - an eternal and infinite life that is fully connected in to God's best plans for us and the planet.

The Leaven of the Pharisees

As the teaching from Luke 12 continues, Jesus' tone changes. The focus of His teaching shifts from His conviction in the way of righteousness to His conviction of the destructive power of judgment. In Luke 12 He warns against what He calls *"the leaven of the Pharisees, which is hypocrisy"*(Luke 12:1). In verse 54-57 Jesus continues:

> *Then He also said to the multitudes, "Whenever you see a cloud rising out of the west, immediately you say, 'A shower is coming'; and so it is. "And when you see the south wind blow, you say, 'There will be hot weather'; and there is. "Hypocrites! You can discern the face of the sky and of the earth, but how is it you do not discern this time? "Yes, and why, even of yourselves (in and of yourselves / in your own power), do you not judge what is right?"*

Jesus draws attention to their abilities to understand the natural world but highlights that a judgment-based operating system causes them to completely miss recognizing an important development in the spirit realm - the arrival of their long-anticipated Messiah. Despite the fact that the Pharisees were highly-trained teachers, their operating system made them completely unable to sense this imminent shift in the spiritual government of the planet. Jesus was about to break open access to God, giving the opportunity to live connected to Him.

Of all the people on earth, the Pharisees were the most aware of the coming Messiah. They lived with this expectation, but now that He lived among them, the judgment-based approach to life meant they could not "*discern this time.*" In verse 57, Jesus is saying, "*When you are separated from God and limited to your own abilities, your judgments do not create righteousness.*" Jesus was distressed by the constricting of their lives caused by the Operating System of Judgment. His heart was to provoke them out of their limitations so they could come alive to Him.

> *Jesus' heart was to provoke the Pharisees out of their limitations so they could come alive to Him.*

Holy Spirit Conviction

The Holy Spirit is the living presence of God, sent to earth after Jesus to reinforce and empower the work God has for people to do on the planet. Jesus said of the Holy Spirit: "*And when He has come, He will convict the world of sin, and of righteousness and of judgment*" (John 16:8). Holy Spirit is released into people's lives to convict us of the same three things Jesus taught about: the destructive power of sin (convicting the world of sin), the absolute highest value of pursuing the life that is possible when we are directly connected into God as a part of His Kingdom (conviction of righteousness), and the futility of living out a life under the power of judgment (conviction of judgment).

In modern Christian tradition, the term "*convict*" is used almost solely for negative awareness. It is not like this for Jesus nor for the Holy Spirit. For them, as it should for us, conviction implies an important understanding of something, like a coming alive to the truth of something as God sees it. In Luke 12, Jesus demonstrates His *conviction* of the power of righteousness (the right ordering of the dominion of God) as He urges ordinary people to overcome their anxiety and trust God into childlike connection.

He tells them that if they will make God's dominion (the Kingdom) their first priority, everything else will be taken care of (Luke 12:31). Jesus expresses conviction of judgment, urging people to stop operating under its harmful power. He points out to the Pharisees what is clear from God's perspective, that operating out of judgment will not connect us in to the way of eternal life and will not produce eternal fruit.

God has disempowered judgment on the planet until the final judgment day (at the very end of time). A whole new way of partnering with His Holy Spirit becomes possible when we understand this. Jesus satisfied the appetite for judgment. He took judgment into His body on the cross. He did it to welcome us into the Kingdom. He gave us the opportunity to grow into a childlike and trusting connection with the Father. Using the Operating System of Judgment as

> *Jesus satisfied the appetite for judgment. He took judgment into His body on the cross. He did it to welcome us into the Kingdom.*

a foundation for life today is in defiance of what Jesus did on the cross. It will pervert, steal, harm, and kill.

Transfer of Judgment

In the Old Testament, in the book of Daniel, the prophet foretold the transfer from the system of judgment.

> "... *The Ancient of Days came, and a judgment was made in favor of the saints of the Most High, and the time came for the saints to possess the kingdom"* (Daniel 7:22).

This "kingdom" mentioned in Daniel is the government of Jesus referred to in Isaiah 9:7:

> "....*The greatness of the kingdoms under the whole heaven, shall be given to the people, the saints of the Most High. His kingdom is an everlasting kingdom, and all dominions shall serve and obey Him*" (Daniel 7:27).

Daniel is saying that a legal decision has been passed in favor of the saints (the people of God). The sentence that could have been handed down for our sin, wasn't. Instead, we were treated as if we were joined to the sacrifice of Jesus and are now alive in His resurrection power, completely free from sin and the Operating System of Judgment.

Hundreds of years later, the Apostle Paul describes the actual release in Colossians 2:

> "*Buried with Him in baptism, in which you also were raised with [Him] through faith in the working of God, who raised Him from the dead. And you, being dead in your trespasses and the uncircumcision of your flesh, He has made alive together with Him, having forgiven you all trespasses, having wiped out the handwriting of requirements that was against us, which*

was contrary to us. And He has taken it out of the way, having nailed it to the cross. Having disarmed principalities and powers, He made a public spectacle of them, triumphing over them in it."

Verse 14 tells of *"Handwriting ... against us."* This is a reference to a legal ordinance. The legal case against us, the sum total of all the loss and harm caused by operating in judgment and our sin, was accounted to Jesus. This amazing moment of spiritual accounting made Jesus into God's legal declaration of righteousness for the whole world. Righteousness, once again, becomes available to all people. Jesus became the cornerstone of the Kingdom of Righteousness, the One on whom the Kingdom of God on earth is founded. Jesus, in His nature as the perfect one, is the highest possible price that could be paid against the cost of sin, unrighteousness, and judgment. When God made Jesus available to pay the full debt of all mankind, this achieved a wholesale shift in the spiritual climate of the cosmos.

Disempowering Judgment

Understanding how Jesus disempowered judgment and completely changed the spiritual dynamics around judgment on the earth is foundational to move into His operating system. Practicing the Operating System of Judgment will keep us believing that judgment is a necessary and legitimate guide to a lifestyle of wisdom. It is nothing of the sort. It is a pernicious force that requires our empowerment to exist as it cuts off our connection to God. Judgment is defiance of all that Jesus paid for.

Father God *imputed/gave/entrusted* all judgment to Jesus (John 5:22). This means that, for a time (until judgment day), the Father gave all responsibility for judgment to Jesus because they had a plan. Jesus would become a delegate of God on earth, living out a perfect human life.

Legally, Jesus did not accrue any liability or debt to evil. Because of this, Jesus was able to use His position of delegated spiritual authority as a circuit breaker in the system of natural law. The human bondage to natural law was finally broken. Jesus' sacrifice became an infinite pool of mercy to swallow up and destroy all of mankind's accrued liability to evil. Because He remained sinless (perfect), His own actions did not create any "*equal and opposite*" reaction. He became a "net importer" of love and life to the planet.

In choosing to die under the power of sin and judgment, Jesus paid an infinite price for the accrued debt of sin and judgment. Judgment and sin's power to imprison and eventually cause eternal separation were offset by the destruction of Jesus, the One who was infinitely good. With this currency of infinite good, God paid the price for any earthly harm ever caused by humans. Doing things in union with God is the only human activity that has an infinite result. Anything else humans do without God, including harm, is finite in spiritual impact.

No matter how much evil gets released into the planet by all the humans who ever live, it is still, as the product of finite beings, a finite sum. Jesus is *infinitely* good. Therefore, He is an infinite price for a finite debt, causing the system to move into infinite credit. This is called mercy, undeserved good. God can allow the cosmos to continue in that state of mercy for as long as He chooses. It is now God's good pleasure to hold judgment off until the very end of time.

> *God has given us the opportunity to live in the infinite mercy that He released onto the planet.*

We can choose to inhabit that mercy by uniting our lives to God through the opportunity Jesus created. There is no need now for anyone to live under "*natural law.*" We do not exist to give the natural realm opportunity to display dominion over us. Rather, we have a connection to God so that through us, He can display His surpassing greatness in this earthly context. God is very slow to anger and His mercy lasts for a long time (Psalm 103:8, 145:8), so we know He is going to make the most of the opportunity Jesus bought Him to pour out His goodness "*on the righteous and the unrighteous*" (Matt.5:45).

The *Bible* tells us that it will only be at Judgment Day that He is reinstated as Judge and, at that time, we will only be judged for one thing; how we responded to the revelation of Jesus.

Developing a Distaste for Judgment

If we realize the high price that Jesus paid to set us free from the cost of operating in judgment, and understand how thoroughly He broke its power, then we should find even the thought of operating in judgment profoundly undesirable. Reinstating this harmful force by choosing a judgment-based operating system is an unnecessary tragedy when we can choose to live instead in the space where God dwells.

This is why Jesus taught us, as His brothers and sisters, not to judge. Jesus warns, "*Judge not, and you shall not be judged. Condemn not, and you shall not be condemned. Forgive, and you will be forgiven*" (Luke 6:37). Further He says, "*Judge not, that you be not judged. For with what judgment you judge, you will be judged; and with the measure you use, it will be measured back to you*" (Matthew 7:1-2).

> *Judgment is defiance of all that Jesus paid for.*

Jesus refused to participate in judgment Himself. He said: "*You judge according to the flesh; I judge no one*" (John 8:15). He goes as far as saying:

> "*If anyone hears My words and does not believe, I do not judge him; for I did not come to judge the world but to save the world. He who rejects Me, and does not receive My words, has that which judges him—the word that I have spoken will judge him in the last day. For I have not spoken on My own authority; but the Father who sent Me gave Me a command, what I should say and what I should speak. And I know that His command is everlasting life. Therefore, whatever I speak, just as the Father has told Me, so I speak*" (John 12:47-50).

When our operating system is based in judgment, several destructive things happen. In addition to hurting people, we also announce the following to the spirit realm:

1. We do not understand that Jesus made a way for us to be free from judgment.
2. We usurp Jesus' role as the deliverer.
3. We believe that judgment is valuable, powerful and effective, putting us in conflict with Jesus.
4. We believe that navigating out of our own judgment-based decision making without Him is more useful than developing our connection with God to the point where we can do and say the things He has for us to do and say.
5. We are available for torment; the spirit realm is allowed to put us "*under guard*" (Galatians 3:23).

Agents of Infinite Mercy

Our role is to live in the infinite mercy that Jesus offers us, to become His agents of mercy. This is the crowning glory of Jesus' life. The result of Jesus' redeeming work was freedom - freedom from sin, death, and judgment. If we practice judgment, we position ourselves in opposition to Jesus' work; the only destination for us then is captivity. Captivity is any limitation other than one set by God for the purpose of achieving His will on earth. Spiritual freedom is a gift from Jesus; Judgment is a ticket to head in the opposite direction, toward captivity. Jesus is clear. Judgment is not for now; mercy is for now.

> *Spiritual freedom is a gift from Jesus; Judgment is a ticket to head in the opposite direction, toward captivity.*

The Apostle Paul made strong statements about Jesus' teaching not to judge.

Romans 2:1 reads:

> *"Therefore you are inexcusable, O man, whoever you are who judge, for in whatever you judge another you condemn yourself; for you who judge practice the same things."*

And then in I Corinthians 4:5:

> *"Therefore judge nothing before the time, until the Lord comes, who will both bring to light the hidden things of darkness and reveal the counsels of the hearts. Then each one's praise will come from God."*

These verses are a reflection of Jesus' teaching in John 12 that the season of judgment has been postponed until Judgment Day. This era of mercy bars us from operating in judgment while the world gets a revelation of Jesus Christ, the redeemer, who sets us free. In I Corinthians 6:7, we are challenged not to let our judgments of how someone has wronged us entangle us back into the Operating System of Judgment:

> *"Now therefore, it is already an utter failure for you that you go to law against one another. Why do you not rather accept wrong? Why do you not rather let yourselves be cheated?"*

Practicing judgment will cause us to come back under the law and "lock horns" with "the adversary"(Matthew 5:25).

Contrast this exhortation with the ways many believers are taught to fight schemes of evil: writing blogs, boycotting movies, protesting directly against perversion, and living in an awareness of what is wrong with other people and systems, and it is evident that the opposite is happening. These are all ways of going head-to-head with evil.

When such efforts are founded on a human assessment (judgment), or a presumption (judgment) of the danger such issues represent, and we value our own understanding (judgment) of what is at stake, those efforts grow from the same roots as the evil they fight, the Tree of the Knowledge of Good and Evil.

God does not need us to butt our heads against evil.

Christian history is scarred with the legacy of strategies devised in the minds of believers who have not known how to manifest God through a living connection to Him. History witnesses the ineffectiveness of our efforts. From the medieval crusades to the way we protest abortion, believers have tried to represent the Father as well as they thought possible, while implementing strategies through an operating system that actually imprisons us and isolates us from a living connection to Him. This is not the legacy of devotion that believers want to write with our lives.

This directly contrasts with divinely-inspired solutions coming through an individual positioned in God. God does not need us to butt our heads against evil. God releases divinely-inspired solutions to people in His timing so that His victories are established. He has thoroughly undermined evil and if we become agents of God, then we get to demonstrate that in all sorts of unforeseen ways. When the children of God move with God, evil schemes shift.

The Schemes of Judgment

In the following story, the Pharisees try to trap Jesus into the Operating System of Judgment. They ask Jesus a question about paying taxes, hoping He will say something rebellious against the Roman or Jewish laws. Jesus sidesteps their complex schemes and gives their system a revelation of the wonder of God, as recorded in Matthew 22:15-22:

> *"Then the Pharisees went and plotted how they might entangle Him in His talk. …. Saying, 'Teacher, we know that You are true, and teach the way of God in truth; nor do You care about anyone, for You do not regard the person of men. Tell us, therefore, what do You think? Is it lawful to pay taxes to Caesar, or not?' But Jesus perceived their wickedness, and said, 'Why do you test Me, you hypocrites? Show Me the tax money.' So they brought Him a denarius. And He said to them, 'Whose image and inscription is this?' They said to Him, 'Caesar's.' And He said to them, "Render therefore to Caesar the things*

*that are Caesar's, and to God the things that are God's." When
they had heard these words, they marveled, and left Him and
went their way."*

The Pharisees had a four-pronged strategy:

•They honored some qualities they admired in   Jesus;
His love and freedom. (*Flattery*)

•They established a connection to truth. (*Legitimacy /
Justification*)

•They presented a situation requiring   resolution.
(*Need*)

•They gave Jesus a chance to join them in making
judgments. (*Opportunity / Invitation*)

See how the Pharisees pointed out how well-suited Jesus was to
the role of a judge? See how they offered Him a place of
authority and explained how the position of an authorized
judge in their system would empower all His best gifts and
character? This is called flattery. They knew that if they could
ensnare Him they would vindicate everything about the system
they had established. Systems and situations with roots in the
Operating System of Judgment will always try to offer us a
place where we are relevant and our gifts are appreciated. The
promise is always that we will do very well there, but no one
born to be a free man does well in a jail.

The Pharisees asked Jesus for an opinion (*Opportunity/
Invitation*). The Operating System of Judgment will always try
to provoke a person to become active in judgment. It will try to
persuade people that their judgments are absolutely essential in
that moment (*Need*). People step into this role with a
seemingly noble cause or opinion and get entrapped in the
system without even realizing it.

There is no question that there is some relationship between "truth" and the Operating System of Judgment. But "truth" can be misused validate a scheme of judgment (***Legitimacy***), and also provide a "reason" to act on it (***Rationalization / Justification***). The devil once attempted to pull Jesus into operating in judgment by quoting Scripture as recorded in Matthew 4:6. This application of "t*ruth*," even when authentically "true," is not living truth. It is not the pathway to life. Jesus (and us) doing and saying what is alive to God in the moment is living truth. Living truth always offers a pathway to life.

If the Operating System of Judgment can connect hearts over technical "truth," then cause people to operate in judgment on any level, it can ultimately pull free people back in under the Operating System of Judgment. It is the very freedom the Pharisees "*praised*" in Jesus that the Operating System of Judgment works to destroy in Jesus' followers.

At the end of this story, Jesus' response to the trickery is inspired by God and provokes wonder in the men who tried to entangle Him. People seeking to harm Him receive a revelation of the greatness of God. He did and said what God had for Him to say in those moments, and people's hearts became inspired by the freedom and the life-giving power that came from Jesus' union with the Father. "*They marveled at His words*" (Matthew 22:22).

When we operate out of our connection to God, we learn how to side-step the opportunities and invitations the Operating System of Judgment brings us. The better we get at doing and saying and thinking what God is thinking in the moment, the closer we get to being able to help set others free, even those whose intent is to cause us harm.

Laws and Systems of Entanglement

Jesus knew that judgment entangles a person into a multi-level system of captivity and punishment. The language He uses to discuss judgment, and the threat it poses, is a mixture of the technical terms assigned to the ruling system created by the Pharisees; "the council," "the magistrate," "the judge," "the jailor," "the officer," "the Sanhedrin," and references to being "under guard" (Matthew 5:25; Luke 12:58). The Sanhedrin was the Jewish governing body, the Supreme Court of Jewish law during the time of Jesus. It was led by a three-member ruling council; a prophetic picture of a false triune godhead.

In Matthew 5:25-26, Jesus listed the dangerous growth in entanglement as we are drawn into schemes of judgment:

> *"Agree with your adversary quickly, while you are on the way with him, lest your adversary deliver you to the judge, the judge hand you over to the officer (hyperetes), and you be thrown into prison. Assuredly, I say to you, you will by no means get out of there till you have paid the last penny."*

Jesus reminds us that if we put so much faith in our own "rightness," we will break relationship with those we should be positioned in love towards. This takes us out of our connection with Him and right back into the system of oppression and captivity.

The Greek word "hyperetes" in verse 25 can mean an "officer" employed to carry out the commands of a higher ruler, or an "under-rower," one who rows under the command of a captain. This connects to the verse in Isaiah 33:21 which prophesies about the New Jerusalem after Jesus: "But there the majestic LORD will be for us a place of broad rivers and streams, in which *no galley with oars will sail*, Nor majestic ships pass by." The galley with oars is a picture of a system that harnesses the power of people to perform a function that God does not require of us.

The Operating System of Judgment makes people slaves.

The Operating System of Judgment makes people "hyperetes," under-rowers or slaves. This enslavement occurs very early in many people's experience with Christianity. Whenever Jesus is presented as a "package deal" that includes the adoption of a set of intellectual or cultural beliefs and behaviors, people can be harnessed into a form of life that is presumed to be "knowing" God; unfortunately, the package deal isn't knowing God. Some examples of package deals would be:

- "Jesus has saved me and now I have to do everything I can to let people know."
- "Now that I am a Christian, every Godly decision I make shows people the value of Christianity and their need for a savior."
- "Christian life is about sharing, loving, and being a community that has different values to the mainstream world."

Whenever people get "saved" into a judgment-based package deal, rather than growing into living relationship with God, the living presence of God is minimalized. To make up for the absence of the living presence of God, other dynamics must be heightened to increase the emotion to a degree that seems appropriate for a major life decision.

Many dynamics are used to create the heightened energy required as people are pressured into a legal arrangement in the name of salvation: fear of going to hell, hatred of the world, the need to be "right," fear of being publicly humiliated (Imagine if God played a movie of every moment of your life on a giant screen in heaven.) These energizing packages of judgment do not disappear after the "salvation" arrangement is enacted.

If the initial decision to give one's life to Jesus comes as a judgment-based package deal, then the initial purpose or direction of the journey as a Christian will be skewed by the appetite of that set of judgments from the outset, making it very hard for a living relationship with God to grow. Instead, an individual will live under a pressure to achieve the outcomes and effects they believe are necessary to demonstrate the power of the original agreement.

(For example, making sure people notice that their values are "different," serving more generously than "unbelievers," etc.) Such an arrangement makes a person a captive to a particular cause, aligns them with an accuser, and gives them a lifetime of slavery, demanding how they must justify the price Jesus paid for their salvation.

Jesus' operating system does not put the burden on us in that way. The Operating System of Jesus releases people from bondage. It does not enslave people to schemes that are conceived outside of the mind of God.

Chapter 6

CHOOSE JESUS, NOT JUDGMENT

How we let God connect to us and love us affects everything we do. When we have permission to get rid of judgments and assumptions about our own personal connection to God, there is a lightness that kick-starts growth. Many people have unkind judgments about their relationship with God which injure the connection and make it unlikely that the connection will be valued and growing. Many people readily access extreme judgments about how God needs them to change and become better; in fact, Christianity often encourages it as a spiritual discipline. Often these ideas are much more accessible and powerful than people's connection to God. These judgments can sound like:

• There is something wrong with me.

• I am a rebel. God can't work through rebels like me.

• I can't expect God to seem close if I am too undisciplined to even study the *Bible.*

• I am not the type of person who feels God.

• I am different than most Christians.

• Beauty inspires me. I must be too worldly for God.

• I think too negatively for God and I get upset easily.

• I cannot do spiritual stuff. I am a practical person.

• I like doing my own thing; God doesn't want that.

> *Jesus is the heart connection with God across which divine empowerment happens.*

It helps to resolve that the voices of accusation will not be allowed to influence us as we allow our heart connection space and time to freely develop. Remember, your infinite heart connection with Father God is actually the Father's gift to Jesus in response to Jesus' prayer, as recorded in John 17. Since it does not belong to us, it is not ours to judge, criticize, or to make demands of what it should look like. If you give God the opportunity for the longed-for-union with *your spirit*, then connection and union will happen.

Once you resolve to stop judging your connection to God, and let God grow the connection from wherever it is toward His infinite relational possibilities, you will get very good at noticing undermining voices for what they are- evil. Ignore them. Walk away from them. Once you cancel your subscription to the Operating System of Judgment, the Holy Spirit is much more obviously available. You will encounter God much more easily outside of jail. Jesus is the heart connection with God across which divine empowerment happens. God's purposes are achieved directly through this connection. We remain vulnerable to Him so the connection stays open and unlimited.

We never get to measure connection to God. We don't get to rate ourselves on a scale of 1 to 10, or describe how our connection to God compares with all the other Christians we know, even in secret. All of that is judgment. Instead, we know that our heart connection has begun, and that it can increase, so we think of it simply as "increasing." Without judgment, we cannot set any limits on how powerful our connection with God will become. Jesus prayed for a complete oneness, that is, an infinite union. As a result, we can cherish our heart's connection with God that is "increasing towards infinite."

Growing Heart Connection

So how can we let our heart connection with Father God grow? With unlimited reverence and unlimited hope for the connection:

> •Ask God to establish it in whatever way He wants. Give Him complete license.
>
> •Refrain from judging yourself or your relationship so that it can grow in peace.
>
> •Notice Him in daily life.
>
> •Remain tender and open.

The heart-connection to God benefits from care. Jesus was described as the one who would not break a bruised reed nor snuff out a dimly burning wick (Isaiah 42:3; Matthew 12:20). Jesus had access to infinite strength but He always acted in ways that made a stronger relationship with Him possible. His strength was never a threat.

> *Jesus' strength was never a threat.*

This is not only Jesus' practice toward a believer's personal connection to Him; it is also His attitude toward the heart connection He has with all people. Every time we decide that we can judge the condition of another person's soul, we are releasing limits and condemnation towards them rather than bringing the strength of God in us to their situation.

The effort God makes to establish a heart connection is far greater than most people expect. It is in His nature as a Father to help us succeed. Once our spirit has connected to Him, God moves from being a passionate pursuer to a jealous lover. He will go to any lengths to get you close, and when He has you, He is ferocious to protect His intimate access to your heart. He is successful and effective. So if you let Him have access to you in whatever way He wants to, the relationship will be established, protected, and empowered by *Him*. It is simpler than we expect. Experiencing a strong connection to God is so compelling that even though disappointment or hardship may come, it is almost impossible to turn away from such a sure source of protection.

If you have not experienced a powerful personal connection to God, hell will use its power from the demonic realm to persuade you any way it can that you are personally disqualified from God's invitation. People sometimes live in quiet torment, believing something is wrong with them because they are unable to access God like others around them. Thankfully, God is not phased by any of your *"disqualifications."* Remember, God's heart is jealous for you. If you choose to honor what He has done by finding you, and what He does then by inhabiting you, holding you, and tending to the union between you and Him, you are partnering with the zealous will of the most powerful being in existence. It works really well.

God continues to increase and develop the joining of us to Him until we experience it for what it is naturally designed to be, the confident foundation of everyday life. From that point on, anything that reduces or damages our connection to the Father can be clearly experienced for what it is—a scheme from hell. People who take time to establish a deep heart-union with God and who tend that relationship, develop a strong spiritual immune system. Even if their mind takes them somewhere momentarily, they have a "short leash" and find themselves being strongly pulled back to a place of righteous union to God. Living with our connection to God as our reference point becomes self-reinforcing. We know ourselves only in our union with Him and, as He moves, the way that He is moving becomes our way too.

A Simple Hug

The woman had described things to me that she never told anyone before. I didn't know what to say. I hugged her, and she buried herself into the hug. The next week at church she told me that when I wrapped my arms around her a stream of love flooded through her and all of the disappointment and shame felt washed away by the living presence of God.

Ali's Story

I spoke to Ali about the fact that she had disqualified herself. I told her how much I could see the goodness of God working through her. Immediately, words came to me that I had not planned to say. I told her that she was just going to put her hands on people and that God would pour through her and heal.

Within two hours, the mother of a young boy approached her for prayer. The boy had been shot through the face accidentally. On both sides of his face, instead of his jawbone, there was a prosthesis. The metal could be felt through the skin, and the boy, John, was in constant pain. Ali put her hand on John and said: "God, thank you for John." Immediately the mother started screaming. Quickly, she ran her hands all over John's face. The metal was gone; the scars were gone. John's face had been completely restored, as if the accident never happened.

Chapter 7

LOVE ENCOUNTERS ANCHOR US

Love is the foundation of the Kingdom of God. Love is a power that motivates people to make themselves, their strengths and opportunities, available for the benefit of another. In relationship with God, all of His strength becomes available to us. His purposes are being fulfilled, but we are the ones who benefit. The experience of Him making His strength practically available to us is an important part of His love.

Ideas about God's love must become a *personal experience of* His love for a transformational relationship with God to actually become real. Perhaps we limit our relationship with God to one of ideas and behaviors because we are afraid that He will not come through if we want more, but God *is* faithful. Scripture tells us that He is faithful (Hebrews 10:23). Don't be afraid to ask for more: more experiencing, more knowing His love.

How we get to encounter God's love is simple: We ask for it. But, the space between us and the encounter is often blocked. There may be a whole wall of opinions and judgments that keep us locked away from knowing His love. However, if we repent of having done, said, or thought anything that has stopped us from knowing God's love, our ability to encounter Him will be restored, and the encounter will come in the form God knows will work best for us. Sometimes we have made judgments or developed ideas when we were kids that lock us out of access to God. Indeed, having been raised in the Operating System of Judgment, it is very likely to be our judgments that determine our limited access to God.

These judgments may be understandably derived from experiences of powerful people or painful years in our lives, but they are still judgments and we need to cancel our relationship with them. Consciously cancelling the judgments we have made that connect us in to the system of imprisonment closes out our sentence. The jailor's permission to hold us away from knowing God is broken if we cancel our association with the judgments we have made. In exchange, we place ourselves with Jesus, the One who paid the cost of all judgment with His blood.

Experiencing His Love

His love can come to us in so many ways. We need open hearts and fresh eyes to see God. Prescribed expectation will always be derived from assumption and will walk us down a path called disappointment. God's love must become a living reality for us. If I tell you that God loves you so much He gave His only Son so that you can be set free from sin and death, it is childlike and healthy for you to give God a personal opportunity to communicate strongly that this love, which was displayed on a dramatic cosmic level, applies specifically to you.

It is not sacrilegious to ask God for a living experience of His love. This longing is not cynical or suspicious. It is childlike to ask for the idea to become your experience. Some people hold back from God, not wanting Him to be offended or disappointed in their lack of faith or understanding. God sees all our limits whether we voice them or not and is not surprised or offended. He paid a high price to establish the reality of a living connection with us on earth. Working through our doubts, fears, and uncertainties is not a problem for Him.

We do not live in biblical accounts and descriptions of His love- its height and depth. Biblical words about the love of God are like title deeds to a house; you still need to open the door and walk in. You can be told you own the house a thousand different ways, but until you move in, it will never be home. You can have a belief that God loves you, and you can back up that belief with all sorts of resources and scriptures, but unless something happens that convinces you to the core of your existence, that you are directly loved by Him, your being "loved" by God will be a technical truth rather than a living reality.

How well do you know His love? Can you feel it? Does God treat you in ways that cause you to feel loved? These are good questions but may be painful for some people. Spending time with God and processing these questions with Him will fast track knowing Him. As we get to know God, we are allowed to pay detailed attention to how He treats us; not just in our circumstances but the living attentions of God to us in those circumstances. How can you believe love is there unless you can recognize His goodness in the way He treats you?

> *His love can come to us in so many ways. We need open hearts and fresh eyes to see God.*

Different personalities are wired to experience the love of God in different ways, some as feelings, others in the form of provision or God's structuring of their life. Do not get fixed on an idea of how experiencing God "should" look for you. The important thing is to know that God does love you, and He will communicate His love in a language that you can receive.

Towards God

After Adam and Eve chose to begin living by their own judgment, they were ashamed and hid from God. A child of God who has chosen to live in His love knows that if we feel shame or anything else that hinders the flow of love and life, we go *towards* God rather than hide from Him; He is always the better option. It is childlike simplicity that qualifies us for the intimacy that allows a love connection to happen. We do not need to strategize, self-promote, or compete for the connection. We do not need to earn it. A strong love connection, in turn, prospers a strong childlike relationship on our end, which naturally allows for the Operating System of Jesus because it is "spiritual common sense" to yield to what God is doing and saying. Jesus said to His disciples: "*If you abide in Me ... abide in My love*" (John 15:7a, 10a). Scripture does not recommend any other way of living.

In John 5:39-42, Jesus says to some Jews who were intent on killing Him, "*You search the Scriptures, for in them you think you have eternal life; and these are they which testify of Me. But you are not willing to come to Me that you may have life... but I know you, that you do not have the love of God in you.*" Having "the love of God in us" happens when we come to Jesus and live into the opportunity he made for us.

It is so simple. Any deficiency, whether in us or our situation, causes us to come to Jesus so that we may be connected into Him and abide in Him. Abiding in Him is abiding in love. As we abide in that love-driven state, our inadequacies are overtaken by His adequacy. Any brokenness we have that is not consistent with Him achieving His purposes will be dealt with as we honestly work with Him. So give Holy Spirit the opportunity to increase your experience of unlimited love. We are instructed to abide in love because God *is* love. Where love is not, He is not. No matter how much we have worked at searching for Him, until we have love, we do not have Him. Keep searching and you *will* find, but do not stop before it is *love* that you have found. When you find it, abide there.

Practical Love

My family was preparing for an international relocation for which we were given only three weeks' notice. One thing weighing on my mind was the suitability of the public school that our two youngest kids were zoned to attend. One of them has more complex learning needs, so I resolved to leave the issue until we arrived as it felt overwhelming.

It was just the kids and I around the last weekend before we left. My husband was travelling. I dropped my kids off at the front of church. It was raining, so I asked them to go in and get seats while I parked the car. I said I would meet them inside.

By the time I got in they had chosen a place to sit, close to, but not our "normal" seats, which were still open. I wondered to myself, "Should we move closer?" Sitting in the seats my kids had chosen, I noticed a friend close-by. I apologized as I leant across the woman next to me, explaining that it was our last Sunday before we moved 8000 miles away, and I wanted to say goodbye to my friend.

I had never met the woman right next to me, but it turned out she was a teacher from the exact school that my kids were zoned to attend in the new country. I was absolutely stunned. We talked after the service, and she gave me all the information I needed to feel confident in that school for my child. I laughed to myself afterwards because I had really been too busy to even ask God for help on this one.

Chapter 8

BELIEF MUST COME ALIVE

The connection between a person and God cannot stay only in the realm of belief. Beliefs that do not lead to union that produces fruit are not life-giving. Be cautious of beliefs that do not come alive in God. They are usually ideas that are being maintained because of a judgment about the value of the idea. Judgments or assumptions about the value of, or need for, particular beliefs are very powerful and very destructive. Such judgments are used to imprison people and their sets of "right" beliefs away from the effective life of "knowing" God. Our opportunity is to be believers who inhabit and are inhabited by God, not people who attach to beliefs and intentionally build culture or tradition around those beliefs.

"I need you to know how hard it is for me to accept this miracle," the woman said to me the day after God had healed the cracked vertebra in her neck. "That crack has not healed properly for twenty years. I only became a therapist because it was the one effective way I found to get pain relief. I wanted to help others get the same level of relief. This miracle undermines all my beliefs." I didn't see the miracle as an undermining, but I was really moved by her candor as she verbalized her struggle to receive something that her beliefs had told her would not happen.

After God inhabits us, we must no longer live exclusively in the realm of belief. We must establish relationship, a different kind of truth that is alive. The dominating nature of the living presence of God is the essential element that drives darkness away and makes demonstration of the Kingdom possible.

John 15 encourages us to move into a life of doing what God has for us to do as He indwells us. The initial belief becomes a habitation: us in God and Him in us. Abide. Love. Produce. It all becomes one seamless process because if we do what God has for us to do, then we are loved and become His. Jesus said, *"If you abide in Me, and My words abide in you, you will ask what you desire, and it shall be done for you"* (John 15:7). In that place, anything that we ask for gets done for us. This happens because we are operating out of oneness with Him, so our desires become one with His.

From Belief to Connection

Earlier we paraphrased John 3:16 as *"....those who trust Jesus enough to fully give themselves into Him and who transition from outside of Him to inside of Him.....will die to the way of death and be married to the One who is without beginning and without end."* It is important that belief in God causes this transition of a person's whole being. We need to know how to live out of a connection with God, like Jesus did. We must abide in God and operate from that place. This is essential. When we first discover a *"truth"* about union with God and the life in God that is possible, we can believe that truth before we have experienced the reality of it for ourselves. We can hear about some aspect of God's nature and choose to believe it is true, but that belief has to lead us to God Himself so that the reality He has for us personally can be established in our lives.

Do I believe infants should be baptized? Do I believe that speaking in tongues is essential for a Christian? Do I believe in a pre-tribulation rapture? Do I believe that women should lead churches? Do I believe it is always God's will to heal? Do I believe that it is wrong to work on the Sabbath? Is that Saturday or Sunday? Put "beliefs" like these on the table and a group of believers can start splitting many ways. Beliefs like these are finite. Any finite belief, even one firmly founded in truth, which does not keep us in the living presence of God, moving with Him, doing and saying alongside Him, slowly pressures the children of light into captivity.

If we highly value our assumptions about God, but we keep Him at a distance, if we focus on how right we are or how wrong someone else is who doesn't agree with us, then we imprison ourselves with these judgments. Our "right" beliefs keep us from the effective life of "knowing" God.

Beliefs are constructs, our best attempts to approach truth. Truth simply is. We navigate in the realm of Truth by following the One who is The Way, The Truth, and The Life: Jesus. We are guided by God Himself, not by our collection of beliefs. We trust God, not what we think about Him. We are held by Him, not because our beliefs are so powerful, but because He is powerful.

> *We navigate in the realm of Truth by following the One who is The Way, The Truth, and The Life: Jesus.*

I choose not to give you a list of all my beliefs because I would rather open a door to a living relationship with God. If I give you a comprehensive set of fixed beliefs, and try to convince you they are right, it might feel like I am giving you a useful guide, something helpful for you to emulate, but, in reality, you would only be looking at a jail of my own particular human understanding. You could either admire or criticize my décor, depending on how much it appeals to you or resembles your own. But if I cannot give you God through Jesus, then all I have for you is human resourcefulness without Him.

Saying and Doing with the Father

Our invitation is to be the people who do and say what the Father is doing and saying. If you feel the pressure to comply with sets of expectations and conventions, if anyone else asks you to determine for yourself what is your purpose or your mission, or tries to determine it for you, if anyone invites you to be part of a distinct identity that builds a wall between you and other people, don't do it. Stay in honor of the relationships around you, but staying in highest honor of your relationship with God means we have less attachment to ideas and more value for the living demonstration of the connection to Him.

As Paul reminds us, *"Now we see as in a mirror dimly"* (1 Corinthians 13:12a). As soon as we narrowly define and lock in an identity and develop a complex set of beliefs and practices around it, we have created a set of limits. This is a polite way of saying that we have become a prisoner. You only want to be the person who, in freedom, and, by choice, stays very close to Jesus and listens to what He is doing and saying, and works along with Him.

People find that the comfort or seeming importance of a strong belief code rapidly falls away when they come alive to doing and saying the things that God is longing to do through them. God has invited us to be His kids. "I am a child of the God who is known as '*I AM*'" is a mind-blowing enough reality. Better not to attach unnecessary beliefs and behaviors to it, so that we are free to actually experience it as God directs.

If you have spent time in a culture that treasures beliefs themselves and their application as distinct from teaching how to know God, you may need time to adjust to the lack of pressure that exists outside of such a demanding belief structure. You will also need courage to believe that your connection to God and your life will grow to fill the space once occupied by that belief system. It will. Kindly, and over time, God will become big to you again.

Sylvia's Story

I was young when I met the sweet person of Jesus. He was beyond description. I loved Him! He loved me! I had met Him! I had seen Him! He was seeing me! My life was fragranced with this devotion, this pure-hearted zeal. I was more alive than my skin could hold.

Soon, I was in ministry. The hunger to hear about this living, loving, real Jesus opened so many doors for me. He and I did it all together. We were a unit, a happy, optimistic, courageous unit. I was beyond secure. I was part of His Bride. I was free from the vote of the crowd. I had met something so good, that my only real problem was not having something big enough to give Him. I felt empowered, passionate, and loved - deeply, deeply loved.

The transition into something I had never asked for was very gradual, and I did not see it coming. My joy slowly decreased and I became really aware of other people and their critiques. Officially, I welcomed the criticism, but deep in my heart it stung me so badly. I tried to stay one step ahead by using constant self-appraisal. I thought of that as my helper- my protection. Intimacy with the Father slipped away. Everyone I loved seemed to be living like this, so I assumed it was the truly Christian way; the mature way. I swallowed it down like chosen, but slightly bitter, medicine. My speaking engagements became all about the relationship I once had with the Savior. That seemed inspiring enough for people who were listening, but I could feel a nagging, hollow ache growing. All I had was yesterday's brightness. This new place offered me nothing. This must be the life of a truly dedicated servant. They are all exhausted, right? What had happened to my passion for prayer and His gorgeous words?

Over some years, my life was purged of everything that was "wrong" or "inappropriate." Whether or not it was pure, or whether it delighted my heart or the Father's heart was irrelevant. There was always a recommendation of how I should change and what shift in emphasis was required. We had such a wealth of considerations to meditate on, including endless discussion and thinking and proposing of ideas. But I lost the Jesus I had so loved. Even the way I imagined the face of Jesus was altered. He grew strict and intolerant. There was obviously nothing left to do except find some additional way to sacrifice. Maybe more effort would win Him back, provoke Him to come closer, cause Him to see my worthiness, my humility, something, anything, I reasoned. I thought of so many things that could be sacrificed, stripping my life down to only duty. I was dying a thousand deaths surrounded by the finest disciplines.

The sacrifices never brought back the connection to God's life that now felt completely gone. Continuing to rise in rank, I was now an enforcer. I, and all that I had been given, was now entwined within a system that totally co-opted my salvation, my God-given gifts and favor. Trapped by a way of operating, and enforcing it all at the same time, my ideals of Christian dedication became heavy weights.

Physically sick and filled with broken emotions, I left the organization I presumed was the cause of the oppression. I tried being part of global reform and looked for God in new ways of doing church, but my way of functioning stayed the same and the ache of separation from God remained.

I had to get unwound. One by one, I broke the commitments I made to a thousand small details that He never asked me to bind myself to. As my connection into His life began to be reestablished, my whole being started to come out of the gray weight that consumed my life. I slowly became the person I once loved to be. He was the Jesus I once loved to love. It came back: the purity, the undivided heart, the devotion. My heart races to think of it: the beating heart of God, uncompromised by other rulers.

The connection to His life is now so strong that I can feel instantly when I do anything that commits me to something that is not Him. The wonder is that the journey into this life place is so very simple and completely accessible. It is the "normal" walk with God – radical life, deep peace, uncrushable joy.

Believe in God, and do what His voice says to do, and you will find that He is incredibly fond of you, and He will make His home in you (John 14:23b), and together you can do extraordinary things. You will live by your connection to Him. Together, you and God will grow "much fruit."

Chapter 9

JESUS IS LIVING TRUTH

When we live inside any paradigm, the boundaries of the paradigm constrict and filter truth and limit its effectiveness. If instead, we live within the Operating System of Jesus, the living Jesus Himself is the infinite truth that inhabits us. Jesus is not a set of ideas and beliefs that we apply to situations. He is living truth, the redemptive Way, Truth, and Life for planet Earth. Many people are taught to give their hearts to "protect truth," or "defend truth," or "live by truth." Of course, "which truth?" and how to live by it is always a product of the Operating System of Judgment. It is an exercise in disappointment and confusion. The living Lord Jesus is Truth; we live and move with Him. He does not need us to defend Him, or protect Him, and if we reason (judge) about Him or create a lifestyle around our value for aspects of Him, we will not stay close to Him.

Many people are raised in cultures that love truth and love Jesus; however, the manner in which truth is taught makes it hard for life-giving fruit to come from their love for Jesus. A sense of stillness eventually comes into many denominations and movements. In a desire to preserve the movement or denomination, people commit to judgments, assumptions, reasoning, or ideas that they believe are essential. That commitment to a set of beliefs builds a jail of judgment. The living reality of God in their lives fades as they become agents representing their special or distinctive qualities rather than direct brokers of the life of God to the world. The living expression of God on this planet becomes better expressed somewhere else.

Ideas of Truth

Some elements within Judaism became fixated on the study of the written word of God. It was considered the ultimate expression of "truth." We must not let our judgment of the value of Scripture cause us to make assumptions about the value of encoding it into our lives. The living Jesus is a higher revelation of truth than any scripture-based, Operating-System-of-Judgment derivative. The love for ideas of truth and the importance of those ideas that we see so highly developed in Jewish cultures were supposed to be replaced in Christian culture with a superior truth. The Living Truth came with a name and a nature, Jesus, who is the living representation of the Father. Why would we be content to adopt an exaltation of written Scripture from Judaism but fail to understand how to practically live out the moment-by-moment desires of the living God who wants to make us His habitation?

> *Jesus is not a set of ideas and beliefs that we apply to situations. He is living truth, the redemptive Way, Truth, and Life for planet Earth.*

Jesus promised that He would never leave us and that He would send the Holy Spirit to guide, help, teach, comfort, and counsel us. We can confidently trust in the ongoing, living presence of Jesus and Holy Spirit in every aspect of our lives. In many churches, a great deal of time and effort goes into studying the Bible and discipling people according to its words, but where is the training to discern and move with the living presence of Jesus? This bias to a book is not the fruit of union with God that Jesus longed for. Our passion for Him, our love connection to Him, and our access to Him as the resurrected Son of God is our way of walking "in truth."

Kate's Story

Kate walked through her house and "saw" Jesus standing next to what appeared to be a gorgeous painting hanging on a section of the wall. She kept that wall blank because she had not found the right painting for it yet, so Jesus had her attention. She watched as He started to explain the painting she could see. It was a painting of her life and her heart, showing intricate details of what God loved about her. Kate fell to the floor and wept because of the nature and power of the encounter. As she lay on the floor weeping, her fifteen-year-old daughter, who had not met Jesus before, walked in and asked what was happening. After her mom explained her encounter with Jesus, the daughter quietly knelt down and said, "I want this God right now!" and she gave her life to Him.

When we live from our connection to God, outside the imprisoning confines of judgment, God's above and beyond, the Living Truth of God Himself has room to happen. This level of access to God is readily available to all people, but many of us live in cultures where this is an exception, cultures which are largely shaped by "static truths." It is time for people to be set free from jails that Jesus cannot inhabit. A corporate culture of "God" will only exist when the main occupation of Christian leaders is knowing God and learning how to move with Him. The Operating System of Judgment and its use of static truth prevents that kind of knowing.

> ## *It is time for people to be set free from jails that Jesus cannot inhabit.*

Static Truths

Static truth is anything with an origin in truth, wisdom, or revelation to which we form an attachment and elevate because of our perception (judgment) of its value. Another name for "static truth" could be "wise principles." Examples are:

- Thankfulness keeps our lives away from the devil and in the Lord's hands.
- Godly decisions are the building blocks of Christian maturity.
- Selfless service is the pathway to promotion.
- Unless it makes you stronger in the Lord it is not from the Lord.
- The most important thing on earth for me is for others to know that I love the Lord Jesus Christ, and I have a desire to introduce Him to them.
- A clear vision is how we measure progress towards our goals.
- God blesses us deeply as we choose to demonstrate biblical love to others.

People accidentally imprison themselves in reduced realities by thinking that their application of beliefs and truths will lead to a closer walk with God. Instead, the practice of belief in their judgment about the value of the static truth starts to steal the life from their relationship with God and walks them back into some degree of lockdown. Under the Operating System of Judgment, a person's energy is dedicated to the particular truth or principle and not to being with and knowing God.

For example, the Book of Proverbs in the Bible will impact a person differently depending on which operating system the reader lives by. Under the O,, Proverbs documents one man's (Solomon's) exploration of who God is and what life on earth looks like when the infinite wisdom of God is available. It is an inspiring book that can draw us into a deep exploration of the nature of God. But depending on the reader, Proverbs could also be a compendium of static ideas and beliefs, turning a written record of God's wisdom into a code of static truth that people try to apply to life under the Operating System of Judgment.

Understanding that Jesus is the living wisdom of God, and that we are always to prefer His living instruction over static truth, takes away the confusion of principle-based Christian living: The problem of knowing which static truth to apply when. Take, for example, these two verses. Are they static truth to apply, or a call to search out the living wisdom of God?

Proverbs 26:4 *Don't answer the foolish arguments of fools, or you will become as foolish as they are.*

Proverbs 26:5 *Be sure to answer the foolish arguments of fools, or they will become wise in their own estimation.* (New Living Translation)

Static truths and sound principles are made available by God to undergird the lives of both believers and unbelievers. We do not despise them; we respect and value them. They are safeguards and boundaries, but they are not the living Jesus or what we should use to direct our lives.

Living Truth

If you think relationship with God can be demonstrated by living according to principle and static truth, consider this allegory: Say you are a law-abiding citizen of the USA. You drive on the right-hand side of the road, you never steal anything, you pay your taxes on time, you voted for the current president. Would you tell your friends you are in a relationship with that president? Technically you are, but it is a distant relationship.

We are not going to experience or demonstrate the living Jesus by living according to principle and static truth that is already widely available in some shape or form throughout every culture on earth.

In the same way, as long as people can be persuaded to group around static truths and stay busy reviewing and studying them, and, with the best intentions, consider how to apply them to the troubles of the world, we will be a people group with only a limited and distant relationship to God. Being a law-abiding citizen will not impress or convince anyone that you are friends with the President.

Being kind to people, because being kind is what believers "do," will not convict anyone of the living power of Jesus, unless, kindness is the living truth that Jesus wants us to enact in that moment. Kindness has some natural power of its own, but if it is merely an expression of your own judgment of how you choose to apply a principle, it will never compare with the power of God at work.

We can look at the Book of Proverbs and see how Solomon was inspired by God to think and write out of wisdom. We can then be inspired to search out God for ourselves and allow God to be our wisdom and anything else that He wants to be through us. On the other hand, we can take the ideas and principles about God and decide how we should present them, and our lives will only show off judgment-based decision-making (the Operating System of Judgment). The Operating System of Judgment reduces good-hearted believers to people who act out good ideas, rather than being a living, visible demonstration of God's goodness.

Goodness of God Demonstrated Through Us

We were doing a simple exercise to activate people in hearing from God. We told people to ask Holy Spirit for three adjectives to describe the person standing opposite them. "Stikcy .um...yeah...um....sweet kind of like a desert.....well actually what I am seeing is this picture of a little girl sitting on the street stirring in all of these ingredients to make the most delicious cakes and deserts" said Bev. The woman opposite her was clearly moved and explained why. As a very small girl, she used to spend time at her grandparents' cake shop, a small street-front shop in old Singapore. She used to help stir the cakes and sweets as they cooked together. God had given Bev words that became a living experience of God's attentive presence in the life of one of His daughters.

I was admiring the work done on the retaining wall when I felt a shooting pain in my lower back. I knew Jesus was wanting to heal someone of lower back pain, so I asked the workmen which one of them had a back injury. None of them said anything. I said, "I know someone has a back injury because I know Jesus wants to heal it." If I was trying to be polite or act respectfully, I would have given up but I was convinced that Jesus was about to heal someone. Four times, I had to insist that I knew that one of them had back pain before finally one of them came forward, revealing that he was in a lot of pain and wore a back brace. Then two more workmen acknowledged that they would like to be healed. All of them were healed immediately and six of the seven workers rededicated themselves to God.

Chapter 10

BREAKING FREE FROM JUDGMENT

Philippians 2:5 states: *"Let this mind be in you which was also in Christ Jesus"*

True Enlightenment

The Operating System of Judgment is the normal operating system of most Westerners - their normal spiritual confinement whether they are believers or not. It is the reason why the West is considered so "closed" spiritually. Western culture raises children in critical thinking and humanism[1], both derivatives of the Operating System of Judgment. If a whole culture can be built out of the Operating System of Judgment, then that culture will be held in a high degree of lockdown away from God. Occurring between the mid-seventeenth and mid-eighteenth centuries, a period known as "The Enlightenment" is often believed to be a time when the Western way of thinking was set free from the constraining presuppositions of theology and superstitions of religion. The Enlightenment is thought to be a turning point in Western thinking into true freedom and clear realities of science.

In all actuality, this period in history involved a shift in focus for the Operating System of Judgment. Prior to The Enlightenment, religion generated most of the parameters for

---

[1] **Humanism** is a group of philosophies and ethical perspectives which emphasize the value and agency of human beings, individually and collectively, and generally prefers individual thought and evidence (rationalism, empiricism), over established doctrine or faith (fideism).

people's judgment-based navigation of life. After The Enlightenment, science became available for people to generate information with which to form their judgments. Irrespective of the time period, both religion and science were used in the same way - as information to enable people to govern themselves through the Operating System of Judgment.

The governmental model was the same; navigation by judgment. Whether religion, superstition, or science generates the "raw materials" for our evidence-based decision-making, the Operating System of Judgment will always corrupt our minds away from God and into limitation. Enlightened Western thinking is a paradigmatic cultural inheritance the same as any other. True enlightenment only comes through minds that are free, moment by moment, to receive from God beyond human understanding.

We Don't Have to Figure Out What We Think Jesus Would Do

In 1896, Charles Sheldon wrote a book called *In His Steps*. The subtitle of this book asks the question "What would Jesus do?" In an attempt to prompt believers to model our lives after Jesus, this question: "WWJD?" is offered to young people around the world. It is an expression of a devotion to the idea of being like Jesus but void of the necessary understanding of how His mind worked and operated.

The hope that we can extrapolate from our own understanding what Jesus would do if He were in our situation, is a good-hearted attempt to translate our faith into behaviors motivated by love. But having to decide what to do, based on our ability to make deductions from studying the accounts of Jesus in the Bible, or deciding what love should look like in certain situations, will not produce anything like the compelling demonstration of the living God that Jesus was.

Jesus' life was not documented for us so we could think about what He did and make assessments, judgments, and assumptions about the right actions so we would know we were modeling our life after Him. Jesus' life was to show us the Father and to make a way for us to "know" the Father like Jesus did, to have our actions guided by our communion with Him. Every time Jesus did or said something He showed us another aspect of God's infinite nature. Jesus came to make a way to God and to demonstrate how to have Him flow through our thoughts and behaviors.

So how did Jesus think? Jesus did not think like a rationalist. Did Jesus review, assess, consider options, and think hard to put things together so that He could work out what God would have Him do or say? There is no evidence that Jesus had to figure anything out or that He ever had to review and decide between options. His mind did not engage assessment, review, comparison, and judgment to lead Him in the way He should go. Jesus thought with the Father from the infinite realm.

There is no evidence that Jesus was "self-conscious" or "strategic" in His thinking. He did not think about how to be a history maker, how He was going to achieve influence, nor did He aim His actions at a plan of reformation. His mind served the one purpose of His life, to know and reveal the Father. This single mindedness gave even His bread making a history-making quality (Matthew 14:15-20).

Jesus' mind was an instrument of communion and knowing. His mind, and the mind of the Father, operated in perfect synchronization. This is the mind of Christ that we are invited to know and to have (1 Corinthians 2:16). This way of "thinking" positions our minds in union with the infinite mind of God so we can bring His nature back into the finite world we inhabit and reveal the true nature of the Father, as Jesus did so perfectly.

Host Disease

In contrast, a mind under the Operating System of Judgment becomes very dominant over its "host person." People with this operating system live most of their conscious life inside their opinions, reasoning, plans, or dreams derived from these considerations. The Christian expression of this mind fits very well alongside humanism because humanism has a similar set of assumptions about the nature and central role of human thinking.

The mind in either case is a constantly whirring machine sorting evidence, opportunities and risks, and imagining possibilities and outcomes. This mind has to constantly weigh options, make "good choices" or even "Godly choices" based on philosophically Christian rational thinking. This mind has to compare and contrast; it has to research, review, make assessments, measure, balance, and eventually, identify goals and strategies to make plans and decisions based on that process.

Believers whose minds are conditioned to operate this way are taught to believe they are thinking in line with God's Kingdom, and even believe that as long as the topic is God, this endlessly whirring machine can help expand God's interests on the earth. There is no record of Jesus ever having a mind like this. Such a state of mind reflects reduced access to God. Jesus never had to work things out in this way because He never lost connection with the Father. He was always able to "know" and never had to "judge."

Invitation to Yada

People get confused about the legacy of the Tree of the Knowledge of Good and Evil, thinking that it gave us our ability to know intellectually or spiritually what is good and what is evil; however, that is not what happened. The devil is the one who invited Adam and Eve into a "yada"-type relationship with good and evil. The fact that the word "yada" is translated into "knowing" does not mean the devil invited them into an intellectual ability to know what is good and what is evil, rather he invited them into the intimate place of "knowing." Humans are built to be creatures of deep and intricate relationship (yada). Much of human intellectual discourse is, in fact, the use of information to prosper **yada with self.**

Like the serpent in the garden deceived Eve, our judgments close off our awareness that it is possible to "yada" God. Jesus had infinite ability. The role of "yada"-type relationship in His life was reserved for the relationship He had with His Father. This was His gift of love to the Father, the demonstration of Jesus' value for Father God. We have the same ability to have a "yada"-level of deeply entwined relationship and our opportunity is to do what Jesus did with that ability - activate it with God.

Some people talk about the idea of "conscience" and say that, as a result of eating from the Tree of the Knowledge of Good and Evil, we now have a "conscience," that our job is to live from our conscience, redeem our conscience, have a sanctified conscience or some other conscience-centered idea. There is no record in Scripture of Jesus having a conscience, nor of God suggesting that we have one either. What humans do have, like Jesus had, is the ability to have relationship with something beyond oneself, one's circumstances, and even beyond the natural realm. It is the ability to have a multidimensional type of intimate and entwined relationship referred to throughout Scripture as "yada."

If we stay connected to God then this knowing is the two-way connection between us and God. This is what it was for Jesus. All of Jesus' earthly life was an expression of the relational oneness He had with the Father. It was an expression of His "yada" with God. If an individual activates himself as the functional godhead, which is what happens when a person uses the Operating System of Judgment, then when he tries to refer outside of himself for "higher" relationship, he will refer to and develop "yada" with the active godhead- himself. Under the Operating System of Judgment, the godhead is a person's own self and their own ability to judge, so they develop yada with themselves. This is the self-referencing that most people describe as the conscience.

Concept of Conscience

There is little surprise that people who live and function in the Operating System of Judgment have a very hard time perceiving God. All of the innate abilities they have that are supposed to be deployed for the purpose of "yada" are being utilized for a relationship with themselves. This is referred to in the Book of Romans. The writer, the Apostle Paul, is trying to puzzle through how it is that leaders can teach one thing and do another. He refers to people "who show the work of the law written in their hearts, their conscience also bearing witness, and between themselves *their* thoughts accusing or else excusing *them*" (Romans 2:15).

> ## "Jesus had infinite ability."

Paul is dealing with a group of people who have stepped out of knowing God into judgments of how their ideas about God should look. This is a glimpse into the tortured and unaccountable reinvention of a prescriptive code that happens inside people when their lives are referenced to their internal judgments or the idea of conscience rather than directly to the living God. The complex realities built by the Operating System of Judgment utilize the idea of a "conscience."

The concept suggests that a person is somehow accountable to a higher good. Paul refers to this voice as "excusing them" (Romans 2:15). It also allows a person's own judgments or their spiritual oppressors to speak into that person's life as the loosely regulated, but completely accessible, voice of "conscience." This is the voice that Paul refers to as "accusing them" (Romans 2:15). The idea of conscience creates a foil for both self-justification and oppression.

It is very helpful to let go of the ideological position that all humans have a "conscience" that is some sort of moral plumb line. In fact, what all people have is some level of "yada" with something. If it is not yada with God, then it is yada with self. How a person expresses the yada relationship with self will be according to ones' chosen values.

When the active godhead is the self, any connection with the spirit realm will either be utilized for benefit or closed off as much as possible. The active godhead will always try to hide how alive and available God is. Anything else would be a threat to its own rule, so the godhead of self seeks to provide all of the answers or application of any spiritual sensing back in the natural realm. This is the realm of earthly ideas and facts, the realm we call "knowledge," in which the self has the most opportunity to display its strength. Mostly this feels to people as if they are working well to do the best job they can of the opportunities they have. It feels strong. It feels important to survival to protect belief in the active godhead. People can be very slow to let go of yada with self. Most people live without an awareness of that being possible.

Yada With Father God

Jesus offers us a far greater opportunity: Yada with Father God. Jesus' strength was displayed when He referred everything He sensed and knew to the Father for direction. In terms of ability to access information spiritually and intellectually, Jesus' "knowing" was unlimited and ours can be too. But what or how much we know is not our strength. Our great opportunity, and the priority of Jesus life was a completely different "knowing". It was a relational entwining called "yada" and He chose to fulfill His ability for "yada" completely between Himself, God the Father, and us, His friends.

Jesus kept Himself completely free of navigating out of judgments founded in experience of good and evil, or judgment founded in having information and understanding of consequences available to Him. Instead, He stayed in complete relational connection with God the Father. Jesus operated in all of the abilities God gave Him, including many different types of "knowing," but the effectiveness of His infinite knowing was because His mind did not school itself in "yada" with judgment, it was dedicated to "yada" knowing of Father God.

Under the direction of Father God, Jesus did and said the most disarming things. In Matthew 15:22-28 in the story of the woman from Canaan who pursued Jesus asking Him to heal her daughter, Jesus is recorded as calling the woman a "little dog" and said that He was not going to help her. This was not in response to some insult on her behalf. It was in response to her worship! The connection Jesus had with His father showed

Him exactly how to provoke great faith and conviction from this woman. She told Jesus that even dogs get crumbs from the Master's table, and this display of great faith got her the result she was going after: The healing of her daughter.

There was no judgment or assessment-based decision-making recorded in the story. Jesus said what the Father had for Him to say, and the woman stepped into realms of faith that were seldom demonstrated to Jesus. Jesus' freedom from "correct" behavior delivered the work of God to this desperate woman. Jesus' connection to God was fully functioning, delivering the divine solution required. Jesus' ability to operate in supernatural knowing was a part of how He stayed one step ahead of His adversaries until the time came for Him to be killed, at which point Jesus gave Himself over to them.

> *The way that God leads us will utilize the gifts He has given us, keep us free, and make us highly effective agents of His light, just as Jesus was.*

In the famous story of Jesus healing the paralyzed man who was lowered down to Him through the roof, we are shown how Jesus used His supernatural connection to the Father to disarm people by responding in words to something they were thinking: **never voiced-only thought.** Jesus announces that the man's sins are forgiven and tells him to get up, roll up his mattress, and walk away. The Pharisees, deeply disturbed that Jesus claimed to have forgiven the man's sins, are caught off guard and challenged even more deeply. The passage in Luke 5:22-23 tells the story well, *"But when Jesus **perceived their thoughts**, He answered and said to them, "Why are you reasoning in your hearts? Which is easier, to say, 'Your sins are forgiven you,' or to say, 'Rise up and walk'?"* Jesus' ability to discern what was happening gave

Him the ability to release the words the Father wanted delivered. The way that God leads us will utilize the gifts He has given us, keep us free, and make us highly effective agents of His light, just as Jesus was.

Connection Void of Judgment

Most people make judgments about their connection to God, that it will be less than what Jesus modeled. We must not do this. If we make assumptions about the limits of our possible connection to God, we can also be tempted to speculate about the value of possible strategies we can use as we move forward without an adequate connection to God. We choose to do things we know will have some effect, and we choose to believe that the resulting effect will be of value to God. Quickly, our faith communities become busy doing things that do not require God.

Any strategy implemented out of assumption or judgment is, by definition, cut out of connection to the infinite nature of God, subject to natural laws; therefore, it will be subject to obsolescence and decline. Maintaining any movement or institution or denomination built on such a foundation will take constant human effort. Those driving the effort will be compelled to harness whatever resources they can from the natural realm to keep moving "forward." This is the picture of the "under-rower" or slave that does not exist in the New Jerusalem (Isaiah 33:21).

Any assumption, judgment, speculation, or considered decision that tries to negotiate between good and evil, achieve a "balance," plot a path of life between two opposing forces, or coerce people to behave according to that judgment, will entrap people, steal from them, and cause them harm. We are not born to generate ideas of our own and dedicate all our strength to turning those ideas into reality. We are born to partner directly with the heart of God as His direct representative. God wants relationship, direct union. We give ourselves to work on His plans with Him, trusting that He will show us how.

Unlimited understanding is available if we pursue it as we would pursue something very valuable to us (Proverbs 2). In intimacy, our minds have constant access to love. In ever-increasing knowing of God, the mind that is loved by God is easily prompted to step into never-before heard or seen words and deeds of God, to see Him manifest in lives, or systems, that until then have been held back from Him.

Robert's Story

Robert, a man in his forties, wanted freedom from some recurring patterns of behavior. He felt that people too easily pushed past his boundaries. In a ministry session, he had a vision of himself as a newborn baby in a hospital nursery crib. Robert could see a "brightness" surrounding him and his crib. He said he knew the brightness was a cloud of God's presence that would stay with him as he lived a life devoted to God.

The vision suddenly switched to another scene. Robert saw himself walking out of the hospital, waving goodbye to Jesus. He was a fully-grown man. Jesus was about two stories tall and stayed behind in the hospital to look after the other babies. There was no "brightness" in sight.

Robert was asked, "Why did you wave goodbye to Jesus?"

"Because I need to do this for Him by myself," Robert said, a little defensively.

The next question invited him to reveal the underlying judgment he was making about himself. "What sort of a person has to do life without Jesus?"

Robert answered despondently but from a deep place in his heart, "An evil one."

At that point Robert's hidden judgment became apparent to him; his "clever reasons" for needing to be without Jesus were exposed as a front for his deeply held belief that he was, by nature, evil. He was then able to step into a future no longer anchored to this destructive judgment, one he had not been conscious of having.

Months later, Robert reported how much his life had changed after being set free from the effect of that one judgment. He did not feel so "available" to anyone and everyone. He felt more respected by his colleagues. He was surprised by how much delight he felt in his children. A father who believes he is evil can suspect his kids might also be "a little bit evil" and parent against that risk, rather than being free to parent from love.

Destructive Judgments

Our most destructive judgments may well be hidden away from our consciousness. We can be strongly loyal to these judgments, function out of them, feel like they are an intrinsic part of us, and not necessarily even know they are there. Despite their hiddenness, these anchoring judgments will influence how we think, experience reality, and make decisions. God can show us these judgments so we can get rid of them.

Often the judgments to which people are most loyal are ones that **were formed early** or which we have formed and recommitted to over time. The process starts when infants and children begin to take in and try to order information. As a civilization, we are still affected by the legacy of the Tree of the

Knowledge of Good and Evil, so navigating through life on the foundation of our judgments is something our children learn to do from a very young age. Any number of factors can influence the type of anchoring judgments people make: personality type, gender, the type of gifts given to a person by God, birth order, nationality, or economic conditions, for some examples. Young humans are inexperienced and vulnerable; they are "sponges" for all the inputs around them, including the judgments of other people, especially older, stronger people.

> *Jesus gives us an opportunity to be "reborn" out of the voices and prescriptions we grew up with and into a relationship that responds above all else to His living voice.*

Some people remember or have been told by their parents about a time in the early years of their lives when they were extremely spiritually aware; seeing angels or demons, or talking conversationally with God. Often adults wonder what happened to this awareness and wish they could get it back. Could it be that the adoption / enculturation into the Operating System of Judgment closes out this awareness of the spirit realm? The child trying to stay safe or work out how to succeed, absorbs the code by which the adults around them live, and develops their own version of it. Adopting the operating system hurts children in different ways, but often the anchors of judgment are deeply buried.

Sometimes, the rules that adults give children are based in wisdom. Sometimes, they reflect the disappointment, the anger, the misunderstanding, or assumptions of the adult. Either way, the directives and opinions we receive in childhood can stay with us forever. Jesus gives us an opportunity to be "reborn" out of the voices and prescriptions we grew up with and into a relationship that responds above all else to His living voice. The value of shedding harmful judgments is obvious, but even well-intentioned rules and principles will become less of a primary source of direction as we let the living God shape our life.

Vicky's Story

Vicky is four years old and lives with her older brother and parents. The gift of mercy runs in the family. They are known for love and kindness. Vicky and her six-year-old brother get along really well. He loves to read stories to her and spend time with her.

During this time, another family of four moves in to the neighborhood. They are extremely wealthy and have different family dynamics than Vicky's family. Vicky becomes friends with their younger child who is also a daughter. The neighbors' six-year-old son is nothing like Vicky's brother; in fact, Vicky finds him loud and moody. Though she doesn't realize it, this boy is a completely "normal" six-year-old boy with a different gift mix than Vicky's brother.

Vicky makes a judgment that the neighbor's son is less kind because he is spoiled since his family has "too much" money. As Vicky grows older, this judgment continues to shape her beliefs. In her walk with God, she is receptive to theology that makes herself the benchmark for how wealthy a believer should be (or not be), and how kindly they should behave. She develops patterns of sabotaging her economic opportunities and exhausting herself by maintaining an extreme standard for the outworking of kindness.

For Christians, as one body, this example is interesting. What happens if a people group who are absolutely inclined towards God's mercy try to live out a commitment to mercy with their own ideas and resources in an operating system that removes the availability of the infinite resources of God? These people would probably choose to live self sacrificially, grow weary, and dissatisfied because they do not have the resources to do all the good they would like to do.

What happens when that group is set next to people with vast wealth? What if the mercy-inclined and exhausted people judge the uber-wealthy individuals by what the mercy-driven people think is "right." What if the "mercy" people create theology or strategy based on their assumption that wealthy people are "self-centered," "not kind enough," or "disinterested in the plight of the vulnerable"? What if gifted business people judge those who are mercy-driven as ignorant of the value of wise stewardship? What if they judge such people as "poor soil" and donate elsewhere? Judgments cause us to create barriers between groups of people. Do you see how the benefit of our strengths and gifts can be withheld from one another by the barriers that judgment creates?

Those strengths and gifts are supposed to all be available to God as He works His detailed ways through us all as one body. When partnered with the Operating System of Judgment, those gifts and resources are entangled into a system that reduces opportunity for divine empowerment, divides people, and causes pain. God can't commission any endeavor that exists to demonstrate the value of the judgments that structure it, no matter how much we want to be doing something for Him. With a foundation in judgment, the effort of believers become no more effective than any caring humanitarian organization.

Part of the wonder of Jesus is that all people, from all walks of life, are drawn to Him. He had no judgments to reduce or distort people experiencing God through Him. When we stop navigating with judgment and let God direct us, we remove ungodly barriers to life and love, causing social and demographic barriers to dissolve.

Sometimes people imagine they will feel lost or unsafe if their judgment-derived road map is removed. This happens because judgments are used by the human spirit to try to find a way forward by locking down variables. This practice partners with fear or vulnerability and offers to reduce the wide-open space and infinite possibilities of life into something apparently more manageable. The draw is a sense of control. It is far better to inhabit infinite possibility with God and let Him reduce your focus onto the specific things He will empower you to do. You are His child; you will experience being led step-by-step into what you are born for.

Most of this book is directed towards a gentle transition out of the Operating System of Judgment, but as you read this next section, invite Holy Spirit to deliver truth in an accelerated, supernatural way. If God Himself can shine light on deeply-held judgments, you will have the opportunity to break your connection and loyalty to them. Once these are gone, it is much easier to transition out of the smaller, less powerful, day-to-day habitual judgments that people make, simply because of being anchored into the operating system and not because they have any deeply entrenched loyalty to them.

The following illustrations are included as prompts for your spirit as it connects with Holy Spirit to hear if there are areas in your life where you can be released from judgment. As you read through them, pay attention to what God is saying and doing in you.

> *When we stop navigating with judgment and let God direct us, we remove barriers to life and love.*

Kristy's Story

Kristy was a highly intelligent woman who studied medicine at a prestigious college. She historically excelled at any subject she took and was ranked in the top five students. She didn't understand why she was driven to perform at such a high level because she was not intrinsically motivated by medicine. Kristy went on to become an orthopedic surgeon. Although, in principle, she loved the idea of being married, she always managed to shrug off men who pursued her. She could not understand why she was so self-reliant. The judgment that <u>God would always be testing her</u> undermined Kristy. She expected that every part of life would be a test.

The compulsion to excel was rooted in fear, as was her distance from men. She existed with a subconscious assumption that men would be like God, a burdensome relationship that would require her to prove herself over and over again.

Ari's Story

Ari was a recovered drug user and former gang member whose lifestyle had been turned around after a supernatural encounter with Jesus. He studied hard in two different ministry schools and was a tireless evangelist. Over several years, his evangelism on the streets led about four hundred people to God. Deep in his heart Ari wanted a simple life, a regular income, and a family, but because of the pain he had caused others in his earlier life, Ari drove himself to "extreme" Christianity, believing that this is what it would take to please God. <u>He believed he must pay God back.</u>

It was a source of distress to Ari that from time to time he yielded to his desire for intimacy and breached his own sexual boundaries. When he gave himself permission to ask God why things weren't working, Holy Spirit showed him that the pressure he put himself under was founded on an assumption that <u>God wouldn't accept him as he was.</u>

Maria's Story

Maria was a manager of a day-care facility for kids across the bay from San Francisco. A series of promptings from the Holy Spirit and some supernatural pointers led to an offer of a position as manager of a day-care facility that was actually in San Francisco itself. The job was an ideal fit for her. She declined the position because she had made a vow to herself that she would never work in San Francisco. She believed that the evil at work in this city was more powerful than God working through her.

Charlotte's Story

When Charlotte was small, another family borrowed her parent's truck to drive to the city. They wrecked the vehicle. Charlotte's parents flippantly remarked to one another, "The city is a dangerous place." Charlotte decided she would never live in a big city. As she grew up, she developed hobbies that required her to live in the country. After graduating from high school, many of her friends left for college but she stayed in the country. Now in her thirties, Charlotte lives a relatively settled life in a medium-sized town two hours from the nearest large city. She is fiercely loyal to her town, and if friends move away she "cuts them off." Charlotte's decisions are based on her foundational assumption that the world, especially in cities, is dangerous. This has compelled her to shape a life within narrow geographical confines that has built frustration and now jealousy into her personal history.

John's Story

In his late fifties, John reflects on his low level of personal "fit" with the profession that he dedicated himself to. He remembers being a young, bright, high school student trying to choose a career path. When the career counselor asked him what he loved, "talking" came to mind, but he remembers censoring his thought. He deliberately *chose not to consider "pleasure" as part of a legitimate way to choose a career. In reality, a role that had included talking with people all day would have utilized his strengths and gifts, but he assumed that <u>anything that gives him that much pleasure couldn't be part of God's plan for him.</u>*

Dave's Story

As an energetic but kind boy, Dave once accidentally hit his sister on the head with a hammer. He lived a relatively happy childhood but always worried that he would hurt people. In his late teens, his first dating relationship failed and the girl was deeply hurt by the breakup, compounding his belief that he would hurt people. In his words, he avoided dating "together" people and only dated "wounded" people. In his early twenties, he started moving around a lot because he did not like to stay with any one social group too long in case he hurt someone. <u>The judgment that he would always hurt people</u> was anchored back as far as his birth. He was told that his mother was injured during his delivery. His disruptive social and geographical transitions wearied and depressed him.

Almost always, our deepest judgments can be traced deeper still to an assumption about God; that He cannot be trusted, that He is unavailable or disinterested in us.

Prayer for Forgiveness and Freedom From Judgment

"God, Thank You for the opportunity through Jesus to bring myself before You without separation. God, I submit my whole self to You, and I ask You to forgive me for my participation in the legacy of the Tree of the Knowledge of Good and Evil. I ask also for forgiveness and release from my involvement in judgment as a guiding power, and I ask that effects of that be removed from my life. God, I ask You to grow me into a childlike ability to trust You. Please teach me directly how to live with You, and from my connection to You, as Jesus did. God would You please establish in me the oneness with You that Jesus prayed for in John 17? I give you full permission to do whatever you need to do to achieve the connection with me that Jesus wanted.

I ask You to release me from the power of any judgments, and preconceptions I have held towards You and any assumptions I have made about Your nature. I did not know better. I ask for forgiveness that I have been more ready to believe what is unsafe, risky, or scary about You than to believe in Your goodness, kindness, and mercy. God, I ask you please to make your goodness and your relentless love real to me. Please reactivate my sensitivity to you, and teach me to recognize you, understand you, and notice what you are doing in the course of my daily life.

I also ask for release from any judgments I have had about people, and this planet and its systems. God, I give you permission and humbly request that You wipe away any damage in my life that has occurred because I accessed the power of judgment to guide myself. Please build my life into the fullness of relationship with You that is possible, and restore my relationships with people and my place on the planet to the fullness of what it could have been if I had followed you in childlike trust. You are the one true God. You are who you say You are, and I thank You for the opportunity to be adopted by You into Your family. Jesus, I welcome the lifetime journey of discovering and living into Your nature. Thank You, Lord. *Amen.*

Created Good

We were created "good" by a good God. It is built into our nature to respond to His goodness. When we operate out of connection to God, we walk in His power, His love, His life, and His peace. Introspection is a process of assessment and review, activities of judgment that imprison us within a self-referenced universe. Instead, we give God as much permission as we can to work through us. As He does, we become like Him. It is impossible for our created natures not to become like the One who created us if we dedicate ourselves to the thoughts, words, and actions of the Creator. *"You are My friends if you do whatever I command you"* (John 15:14). The upgrade of our nature comes as we build a relational history with God. We are invited to stop making judgments about our own nature. Jesus died to create our opportunity to let go of these judgments.

If we choose to operate as judges of ourselves, we step outside of the effect of what Jesus did. Instead, we now let God be our governor and that defines our effective nature; our nature becomes Him. As we walk in obedience, trusting that He can lead us into the highest fulfillment of us, we get to know Him more. The more attention we pay to Him, and the more implicitly we learn to do and say what He is doing and saying, the more the world will see Father God through us.

If we remove the Operating System of Judgment and all its mechanisms of imprisonment from our lives, the life of doing and saying what God is doing and saying will keep us in a holy journey. We will be pulled closer and closer to God. The Operating System of Jesus takes us deep into God's nature. That process of going further and further into Him must not be limited by us deciding "what is right" or "what level of sanctification happens when..." We must not set limits on what is "reasonable," "possible," or "to be expected" of a person. In God, anything is possible. God is the only one who is able to transform us into His new creation sons and daughters. Amazing things happen when we let Him decide how much and how rapidly and to what degree we can be transformed.

Chapter 11

JESUS' COMMUNICATION

Jesus modeled communication that was "out of the box." In order to help discuss *how* Jesus communicated, we want to keep the definition of communication as broad as possible. Let's define it as: the process of transmitting anything (an object, device, substance, or concept) from one being to another, in any way. Keeping the definition this broad means that it can encompass objects like new healthy body tissue (in the case of a miracle) and "devices" like a comment or a command that provokes supernatural faith, or delivers people from demonic oppression. Jesus communication worked as a transmission system for the living nature and power of God. Jesus possessed clarity to communicate on God's terms so these gifts from God would get through the barriers the Operating System of Judgment created.

The Pharisees were offended by much of Jesus' communication. Particularly offensive were the occasions when Jesus spoke in ways that suggested forgiveness from God was released. People who were open to His power travelled great distances to get Jesus to speak a word that would heal their dying children or servants, even when the sick person was in another town (Jesus heals the centurion's servant Luke 7:2-10). Jesus did not reference His communication to the expectations or restrictions around Him. He communicated exactly as the Father asked Him to. His communication achieved divine outcomes because it was in exact and precise alignment with what the Father wanted done.

> *Anchoring our communication to the Father brings it into alignment with God's living purposes.*

127

To most people, communication that conforms to a set of expectations and social norms feels "right" and familiar. Communication in the Operating System of Judgment is usually coded to achieve a certain purpose or outcome - as intended or required by the people communicating. Any communication that is bound to a culturally agreed on code, grafts the person communicating, into the paradigm. This automatically reinforces the core assumptions and judgments that create the paradigm. In that sense, communication that could be assessed as "highly effective" by how well it serves our purposes, will also be highly effective at reinforcing the limits, assumptions, and intellectual bondages of the paradigm in which that communication took place.

Operating Within Limits

Communication in the Operating System of Judgment is harnessed to achieve outcomes that are pre-understood. This process dictates that communication will comply with the limits of the paradigm. Simply put, if we ensure that our communication always functions "well" according to our goals, expectations, and purposes, we will be communicating within the encoded spiritual ecosystem of a paradigm. This communication is part of the active creation, maintenance, and ongoing spiritual perpetration of the limits of the paradigm. It creates, maintains, and extends the barriers between people and God. Our communication becomes harnessed to help banish God from the territory that is under the paradigm. Anchoring our communication to the Father sets it free from the demands of the paradigm and brings it into alignment with God's living purposes.

In His earthly life, Jesus' communication was not limited by the codes and expectations of those around Him because nothing Jesus did supported nor reinforced the limited paradigm that determined their reality. Jesus was present among people to demonstrate access to a completely limitless reality, Father God, and to start to build a Kingdom by communicating in a way that released the actual substance and nature of God into situations and circumstances around Him. Jesus communicated according to the precise design of Father God because His communication was designed to "carry" more than was currently accessible to those who inhabited the lesser reality of the Operating System of Judgment. Whether His communication was transferring miracles, forgiveness, or other freedom, this ability to communicate in ways that transferred redemption directly from God into the natural realm was a direct product of Jesus' operating system. In His communication, Jesus stuck precisely to the score written by His Dad.

> *Any form of communication can be a vehicle that transmits the living power of God.*

Any form of communication can be a vehicle that transmits the living power of God. If we communicate out of a growing "yada" with God, then His resurrection power and miracles can be delivered through our communication. In order to learn to communicate this way, we have to both adopt, and adapt to, the idea that all communication "carries" a spiritual dimension.

Musical Connections

The concept of communication having a spiritual dimension or power, is not an unfamiliar one. Most people will have a knowing of this when they listen to a particular piece of music. Music is a good example of a form of communication that is widely experienced by people to carry profound spiritual power. Once an individual opens up to a piece of music, it can displace their other emotional, intellectual, and spiritual inputs, causing an effect that lasts at least until the music stops. Depending on how quickly the individual reinstates their previous spiritual conditions, the effect of the music can last a long time, even effecting permanent change.

Music is a universally acknowledged phenomenon. Its power originates in God. It has the imprint of His nature and that imprint makes it more than just "sound" or "noise." Unlike other sound, music has structure, harmony, and cohesion. Harmony is a range of notes united into one sound. A chord is made up of three notes in harmony: a sensitive expression of order. Music has perhaps been protected to some degree from imprisonment to the Operating System of Judgment because it bypasses the mind and communicates directly with the human spirit; a spirit created to know God.

The example we have in music hints at what is possible in the Operating System of Jesus. As with music, communication that originates in God can displace any reality that does not conform to God's purposes. A person who is spiritually under the power of one set of influences can have those influences displaced. Some aspect of God's nature, communicated through one of His children, can be delivered in the exact way needed to cause a person's spirit to be open to God and receive from Him.

Most people know that music can change their spiritual and emotional condition, but few people have experienced communication designed by God and graced with His living power to achieve divine purposes. Such communication is alive and powerful. Such powerful communication was normal for Jesus and can become normal for us too. If we allow our communication to be orchestrated by God rather than designed in reference to the encoded norms of the Operating System of Judgment, it will be graced with His nature and power. We will assuredly see supernatural outcomes happen through our communication just as they did for Jesus.

Intimate Communion

If we give this God-laden communication permission to flow freely, then moments of powerful connection lead us into a lifestyle of intimate *communion*. The communication is the joining or uniting, us to God and to one another. This creates bonds between us and God, and ourselves and others that are the living union Jesus asked for. It establishes an eternal legacy of infinite worth. Simple acts and words of communication become the perfecting of the Bride of Christ, the establishment of an eternal and infinite communion.

It is almost always our simple obedience to say what God has for us to say, or do what He has for us to do, that that will carry God's living presence into the natural world. The development of our communication starts with individual elements of connection across which we touch God. These can include a single word that we hear clearly from God, or a complex stream of encouragement. It could be a particularly luminous moment of prayer or a prophecy. These events are more powerful than we can conceive intellectually, and will bring something alive that is far bigger than us.

People often get locked down or stuck over any aspect of communication with God. Remember, that "hearing God" is an English language description of a spiritual process. Any aspect of your body, mind, or spirit can "hear" from God in any way. If you are a visual spatial thinker, you may have had a vivid pictorial imagination all your life. Turned toward God, this becomes the capacity to "see" in the spirit. An auditory sequential thinker may be less inclined to see visions, but may have God-inspired thinking or hear words from Him.

> *Remember, that "hearing God" is an English language description of a spiritual process.*

It is possible to feel God in your body. Some people experience feelings in their core that are a "knowing" or a recognition that something is from God. Some people are deeply intuitive and naturally "flow" in communication with God. Others have to develop one aspect of their life in God over a long time and may never be able to "perform" their connection the way someone else might expect. Free of the constraints of judgment, people can have the courage to "flow" in whatever aspects of connection are native to them. Experiencing how we communicate and having permission to communicate with God in the way He designed us to, leads quickly to a life of being one with God.

What Did Jesus Say and How Did He Say It?

Let's examine some aspects of how Jesus communicated, and what He taught us about communication with the Father. Both of these are a gateway to His infinite nature and the delivery system of Him to the planet around us.

PRAYER

Jesus did not focus on teaching about prayer. This could be because He lived in a state of connection to the Father. Everything He thought, said, and did was from His union with the Father. Jesus' most famous teaching on how to pray was prompted by an enquiry from the disciples. If we look at Jesus' brief response to the disciples' question, we see how, as with everything Jesus modeled, it is an invitation into intimate union. According to Luke 11:1, one of Jesus' disciples asked Him, *"Teach us Lord how to pray."* Jesus' response was:

> *"When you pray, say: Our Father in heaven, Hallowed be Your name. Your kingdom come, Your will be done on earth as [it is] in heaven. Give us day by day our daily bread.*
>
> *And forgive us our sins, for we also forgive everyone who is indebted to us. And do not lead us into temptation, but deliver us from the evil one"* (Luke 11:2-4).

> *God's will in Heaven is uncontested.*

Looking at this prayer in light of an operating system helps us to see how the fruit of this simple prayer can be infinite. If we live the Operating System of Jesus then this prayer covers all of life. We pray to be free from entanglement with sin, fully delivered from the power of evil, forgiven, provided for, and operating as fully effective agents of the advancing Kingdom of God. In the line, *"Your will be done on earth as it is in Heaven,"* Jesus describes the fruit of intimate union with God.

In Heaven, God's will is done in an environment that contains no barrier to it. God's will in Heaven is uncontested. There is no alternate government in Heaven and because everything there is fully aligned with the nature of God, there is complete resonance with what God is doing. Everything is compelled into alignment with God by the power of His presence. For God's will to be done on the earth as precisely and convictingly as it **is in Heaven**, a certain bridge is required; human beings who are connected to God. W*e* have to choose to live from our connection with God.

133

God's plan was always that people would be grafted in to the legacy of Jesus' life, and carry on the work Jesus started. Unless we train ourselves into His ways and train ourselves to move with Him as Jesus did, then God's will won't be done "*on earth as it is in Heaven.*" It will be severely contested, displaying all the hallmarks of a battle, not the clear and precise picture of the nature of Father God that Jesus displayed. If the earth is to see the uncontested demonstrations of God that Jesus was able to display, we have to come into oneness with God. Jesus' answer to the disciples question about prayer invited them into alignment with God's model.

Ultimately, if all God's people learn to demonstrate the Father as He is, all people on earth could live close to a convicting revelation of God in the same way that all the living creatures in Heaven do. The reason the Lord's Prayer is simple and comprehensive is not so that we don't pray anything else. It is simply because it opens up connection and positions us expectant and ready for what God is about to do. Like so many of Jesus' words, it is an invitation into an ever-growing journey with Him.

Praying for Restored Vision

I once prayed for a friend who had 75% vision loss due to burst blood vessels at the back of his eyes. I prayed for him periodically for over a year, but the blindness kept increasing. Then, the situation got desperate, and I began praying for him fairly constantly for a week. I felt a distinct breakthrough when I was by myself praying and heard specific very silly sounding words to pray. I felt led to wash my hands like windshield wipers across the air in front of me. I was prepared to do whatever God showed me to do.

I did not know it, but my friend was booked in for surgery. He told me that as he had walked up the steps to the eye clinic, he had realized his eyesight seemed clear. Inside the clinic, the surgeon took new images of the eyes in preparation for the surgery. When the images showed no evidence of a problem, the doctor thought the machine must be faulty. He fired up an old machine and took a second set of images. The images revealed evidence of scar tissue where bleeding once was, but the bleeding and the blood clots were completely gone. The surgeon said that he had never seen what he was looking at on those images. As far as he knew, it wasn't possible for a change like that to have occurred. My friend's healing mean the livelihood of his family was preserved; they were very thankful to God.

Prayer comes alive as we live from our connection to God. As prayer works through us, we will also be nourished by it. Prayer becomes like a stream flowing through the center of a private courtyard garden, producing life that nourishes the person who owns the garden even as they grow fruit for the surrounding community. Staying free from the Operating System of Judgment, and allowing prayer to be whatever God wants it to be makes it a direct supply of spiritual nutrients – an inner access to infinite life, no matter what circumstances we are in.

THE SPOKEN WORDS

It was not just Jesus' prayer life that had the disciples asking questions. Jesus was known as one of the most confounding speakers of all time. His words drew people but were confusing to those who lived immersed in the Operating System of Judgment. They could not understand Him. Some people hated Him for what He said. Jesus did not exhaust Himself with debate, although He willingly graced the Pharisees with

His wisdom when they tried to argue with Him. Jesus was loved by many for His words.

Tens of thousands would follow Him into the wilderness to hear Him speak. There had never been another person who spoke like Him, but Jesus did not expect to be the last person to be able to speak words directly from the Father. He expected those who followed Him would similarly know how to speak words of life from God (John 6:68). Unfortunately, there is so much mystery, fear, and assumption about the idea of hearing from God, that people using their senses to "know" God and speak words from Him has been a very restricted art form.

The way Jesus spoke, including the words He used and when He used them, was directly under the instruction of the Father. His words were specifically designed by God to achieve a certain purpose. Jesus spoke in strange ways: John 8:6b *"But Jesus stooped down and wrote on the ground with His finger, as though He did not hear."* Jesus told us that He **did** and **said** what the Father was doing and saying (John 5:19). The emphasis was not on feeling the Father's feelings. The special emphasis was on speaking the words of the Father because words are an important way the resurrection power of God is transmitted.

Words of God, spoken by His children, cause a release of power that creates life or *"yields fruit"* (John 15:5). For this reason, how we communicate is important. The Bible tells us that *"the power of death and life are in the tongue"* (Proverbs 18:21). The tongue that speaks words from God creates life. The tongue that obeys the judge in a person's spirit creates prisons, tries to coerce others into those prisons, and partners with decline. Whatever our intent, the words we speak will be serving the agenda of our operating system. How we communicate will change as we learn to speak from our connection to Father God.

Fishing in Someone Else's River

God once gave me words for a pastor I had just met. I told him that he felt like he was "fishing in someone else's river." I continued, "But God says that you are supposed to be there, and it is your river now."

I did not have a clue what this meant but found out later that the man had inherited the large church his father established. He felt unqualified for the position and stayed in his father's shadow. God wanted him to know that he was in the right place.

Front Row Seats

One afternoon, I participated as a visitor in a church's after-school program in a very poor neighborhood. I don't have a natural affinity for kids' programs, so I was feeling out of place. I asked God to bring me someone to love. "Just give me one person I can lock onto!" was my prayer. In a matter of minutes, a small boy about ten years of age was alternately assuring me that he was ready to go to hell and banging his head into a concrete block wall. I knew right away God had sent me someone to love.

The boy was extremely hostile. He was saying things like, "I hate Jesus. I love hell, and I want to go to hell." I stayed with him for the entire afternoon, saying very little. He would not let me touch him. He would not let me pray for him. He was jumpy and disruptive. He was kind to no one. Afterwards, I learned that he was tormented at night and never slept well. If that wasn't enough, his volatile behavior kept him from having friends. He was considered a problem at school and was not allowed to participate in activities like field trips.

Without bothering him, I sat as near to him as I could, often with my arm around the back of his chair. I trusted that Holy Spirit in me would have an effect on him, even though he resisted all my actions. I kept an ongoing conversation with God about His heart for this boy's freedom. We sat like that for at least an hour, chatting a bit and munching on snacks. Just before the session was over, I drew him a picture. I told him it was from God. I asked God what to draw, and God showed me the face of a lion and the words "My eyes are on you." I drew it with the boy watching me intently. Then, I heard the voice of a previously disruptive kid whisper, "I am going to cherish this."

I moved on to another town that evening, but a report came back to me. The boy slept peacefully through the night with the picture of the lion's face next to his bed. By the end of the week, he received the award at his school for the most improved student of the week, and, one year later, I heard that he was no longer restricted from field trips. All the disruptive behavior stopped. Despite the fact that I did not have any idea what God was going to achieve, I used the Operating System of Jesus. I felt connected to God, and I did what I sensed He wanted me to do. Somehow in that process, God had a profound and moving impact on that boy. God can deliver Himself any way He likes, but the Operating System of Jesus is a really good way to get peaceful front row seats.

Not a Good Listener

Jesus was not a "good listener." There is very little record of Him listening to anyone. He did notice whether people were grumbling or making requests. He had good hearing. But, in the modern social sense, He was not a "good listener" even when surrounded by a small number of people. Why? Because He was confident that what He had to offer was important and that He would deliver it well. This was not arrogance. It was a feature of the power of His connection to the Father. Jesus had words that were a direct connection to Father God for the people around Him.

God's words compel. When Jesus spoke God's words, His followers were compelled to listen. The disciples expressed it like this: "*Lord, to whom shall we go? You have the words of eternal life*" (John 6:68). If a person becomes excellent at saying what the Father is saying, God's presence in those words makes them worth listening to.

What can we deliver when we yield our communication to the Operating System of Jesus?

•Encouragement.

•Inspired teaching.

•Prophecy.

•Words of knowledge for healing, breakthrough, knowing the heart of God.[2]

•Words of reconciliation (clear illumination of the way of life and love in a situation) for people to each other and people to God.

•Words of wisdom.

•Ideas and inspiration from God. Sometimes He wants to talk about things that are hundreds of years into the future. Leonardo Da Vinci drew his helicopter long before they were built and flown.

---

[2] Word of Knowledge – from 1 Corinthians 12:8– Is a spiritual gift of insight or revelation about a specific situation that is received from Holy Spirit through any of the senses.

139

As we establish a history of trust in God, we progressively become people who live by the voice of God. Once this is normal for us, it becomes easy to listen to God in every situation.

THE STILL SMALL VOICE

God's "STILL, SMALL VOICE" (1 Kings 19:12) (*an ancient term for words communicated directly from God as thoughts into our minds*) gives us immediate access to thoughts authored by the Creator of the cosmos. We learn to notice the still, small voice of God because it usually comes as a sudden thought out of nowhere with no apparent train of thought leading up to it. It is important to realize that anything in the spirit realm can prompt us to have "thoughts." Angels can deliver messages as thoughts and, over time, we can learn to discern the difference between angelic messengers and the Holy Spirit.

Communication from demons can arrive in the same way, as fully formed thoughts, although the nature of the messages is vastly different. Demons often betray their presence by the nature of the thinking that spontaneously happens when they are around. If our judgments or commitment to static principles "match up" with demonic activity, then that demonic pressure will be "noiseless" to us. It will hide behind the limits of our judgment-constructed "realities" or behind commitment to static principles.

People often have a large number of small judgments that legitimize the active communication from the demonic realm and exacerbate our inability to hear God. This clouding of our access to the spirit realm is designed within the Operating System of Judgment to preserve separation from God. Whether it is promoting our connection to strategy that displaces God's living input or justifying the absence of God's voice, the Operating System of Judgment will do anything it can to prevent us from communicating with God in the free and expansive reality of the Operating System of Jesus.

God has given us communication tools that break people out of these constraints. The so-called "languages of the Holy Spirit" or "speaking in tongues" is a phenomenon established by Holy Spirit so He can work directly through us in a way that completely bypasses possible interference from our intellect. The Holy Spirit uses this remarkable union between God and people to release sound that achieves His purposes. Speaking in tongues frees our faculty of speech from the direct control of our intellect.

Speaking in tongues, often and for extended periods, is a highly effective way of unlocking people into union with God. The practice allows God to release words through us to achieve any purpose. God's nature is so geared towards connection that He will often use our praying in tongues to cause us to grow more fluent in His ways. Praying in tongues is also, unsurprisingly, a type of communication that is extremely awkward for people who are locked down by the Operating System of Judgment. Accessing this private treasure of connection to God in this way requires us to allow our ability to speak to be set free from any judgment-derived "grid."

Getting the Message

Someone once had a word from God for me. It was, "God likes how you like watching the grass grow." The person who delivered that word was being childlike and trusting. It meant nothing to them. They thought there was a good chance I would think the word was ridiculous. In fact, the word meant a lot to me. I love agriculture and soil microbiology, and, at the time, I lived on acreage and enjoyed walking the fields and observing the details of how pastures grow. Once, as I was out walking, God commented to me how much He liked how I looked at the details of the blades of grass. A few months earlier, yet another person had shared their vision. In it, Jesus and I were walking as friends across a field and stooping down to observe the details of how the grass was growing.

The person who had the courage to tell me "God likes how you like watching the grass grow" was used by God to encourage me in a private language of which they had no understanding. They faithfully delivered what they had.

VISIONS

God also speaks through VISIONS. He is light and His angels are "ministers of light," so painting pictures with light is part of the nature of God and His angelic assistants. These glimpses mostly come as images across our "mind's eye." In the same way that revelation from God usually comes without a thought trail leading to it, visions are more clearly from God when they are not part of a journey of our imagination, or we have not daydreamed our way into the vision. However, visual messages from God do not always have to be isolated or disconnected. It is possible to develop great "visual intimacy" with the Lord and see constantly unfolding vision language. The "seer" gift, or the ability to see in the spirit, enables a person to live in a perpetual flow of this visual language of God.

Nicole's Story

I prayed with a young person who really wanted her lifestyle to include a higher level of trust in God. This woman's past included physical abuse and a friend being murdered. These events were still woven into her present in a way that was very hard for her to negotiate. We prayed, but I still felt heaviness, so I asked God what He wanted to do.

I asked the woman "Do you still see Jesus?" She said that she did, right next to her. Then I asked the words that just dropped into my spirit, "How big is Jesus?" "About as big as me," she replied. Then suddenly she gasped, "Oh," obviously surprised. "Oh! What is this? Oh, I have never felt this before. This is so real!" She got down from her chair and curled up on the floor in a little ball, snuggling into the carpet like something in a nest. A few minutes later she explained that she had gone from having a face-to-face conversation with Jesus to being like a tiny little baby the size of an acorn, snuggled down deeply into Jesus hand, and feeling so very safe.

Traumatic events of the past had heightened her self-protective instincts. This self-reliance prevented her from being able to access the support that God wanted to give her. The question God gave me, "How big is Jesus?" led her into an experience of something that trauma had defaulted her out of; being a small child held by a powerful God.

Emma's Story

Emma lives in a city with a high level of unemployment, especially among the youth. Many of these young people hang out on the streets at night, drinking and experimenting with drugs. Emma hangs out with them, loves them, and prays with them. Usually when she goes out, fifty or so of these teenagers gather to be with her. The night I joined her, I was really looking forward to seeing what God would do.

At one point, a drunk teenager called me an idiot. The Holy Spirit replied to his drunken, off-handed remark by giving me a word about how despised this kid was in his family. I said to him, "I am not an idiot and neither are you. You were called an idiot by your family when you were little..." God then gave me a very clear picture of his family and details of the banter between his dad and his siblings that had hurt him so deeply. I continued without stopping, telling him what God was showing me about how his mind worked, that he was a very bright thinker and how he thought in solutions and possibility rather than obstacles. I spoke of the value of this way of thinking.

This guy and a few of his buddies standing around him became instantly sober. The hunger in them for the words of life we were delivering pulled their body chemistry out of the dominion of darkness and into the clear light of Jesus. In that state, they were compelled by the kindness of God and several of them came into relationship with God that night. One of the young guys was filled with the Holy Spirit, and the feeling was so surprising to him that he went and hid behind the nearest parked car until he adapted to his new awareness of God.

A heart of love and a yielded life allow us to be positioned in honor, so God can speak whatever He wants through us to produce fruit only He can produce. Our ability to communicate must get released from the norms of the Operating System of Judgment into God's superior realities. You have full permission to hear directly from God, and you are all the equipment necessary to hear from God. Your whole body and senses are a receiving device that can "hear" and be led by God so that you can do and say and think what God has for you.

> *You have full permission to hear directly from God.*

A Healing Hug

I was out one night with a friend, and we had a word of knowledge for a homeless man's knee. He let my friend pray for him but didn't want us to check to see if his knee had been healed. He spoke with resigned acceptance of his 'broken body.' I looked at this man and saw despondency collected on him, like trash that wasn't really a part of him. I saw the word 'hug' written over him and couldn't get it out of my head. We chatted and I found out his name was the same as my middle name. I leaned forward with my hand out and introduced myself properly. He pulled me in, so I grabbed his upper chest and neck and hugged him pretty tightly, speaking words over him as I did so—like a proud dad after a kid's valiant effort at a football game.

The hug continued for what felt like minutes. As we let go of each other, I asked him how he was, and he said his neck was pain free and unlocked, his lower back was pain free and not stiff anymore, and the carpal tunnel pain in his wrists was gone. He got up and left his cane behind as he went for a walk! As we allowed ourselves to be freely with God, God was freely Himself through us.

Randall's Story

One day, I was talking to a thirty-something-year-old guy. It was only the second time I had spoken to him, and I was thinking that it would have to be my last. Every word he said seemed so contrived, so "perfect" and "fake." My level of frustration was unacceptable to me, so, as I chatted along with him, I pleaded with God. "Please give me the words!"

God immediately said, "Ask him, 'Do you review your words before you say them?'"

"I review every single word before I say it" said the man. "I have done that for as long as I remember."

145

"Do you know that you don't have to do that? That you can get rid of that pressure?" He thought the idea was wonderful but wasn't convinced it could be possible. We discussed things a bit more, and I explained to him about torment. I saw him three days later, and he was a changed man. He was free and beginning what turned out to be a deeply intimate journey with God.

The eyes of our spirits are powerful. Our minds regulate (often choosing to shut down completely) the inputs we receive from our spirits. We justify the practice of ignoring the things our spirits can see by ascribing higher value to the activity of the intellect. Choosing to pay attention to glimpses in the spirit realm rather than ignore them, will rekindle our ability to "see" what is going on in the spirit realm. This will lead us to a much more expansive awareness of God's realities very quickly.

> *Visions can be an important part of how God makes Himself available through you, to the planet He loves.*

A Place of Healing

One day, God pointed out a woman in a crowd. Later that day, she approached me and asked for prayer. I put my hand on her head and in my mind's eye I "saw" a sky-blue space far above the clouds. A bright shard of light entered the space. At that prompt from God, I said in my spirit to Him, "I release my sister into the place you have for her." Her legs gave way and we helped lay her down. I knelt beside her and heard angelic singing, so I sang along quietly. After about five minutes of singing, I left and another believer stayed with her. The following day that woman found me. She had been healed of a life-long learning disability. Prior to the healing, she *would read a page of a book, turn away to talk to someone for thirty seconds and have absolutely no recall of what she read just minutes before. After her healing, she went home and read all night long and remembered all of it. She was so happy.*

She said that when I put my hand on her head she had "seen" a bright blue light, and suddenly felt like she was floating on the clouds and everything turned blue. She continued telling what had happened with a breathless joy, "I don't know if you were singing or if it was angels, but I was surrounded by the most beautiful singing." I was thrilled. God had given me a vision of a place of His presence where He would heal His daughter. That place had come alive to her through my unspoken prayer.

DREAMING WITH GOD

God designed us to put aside our consciousness as we sleep and be receptive to His spirit through DREAMS. Many of us sleep through our dreams and pay little attention to them. When God wakes you from your sleep at a specific time to cause you to remember a dream, you should pay attention to what He is saying. If you write your dreams down, it will become a valuable reference. God can reveal the significance of your dreams over time. Dreams can come from God to reveal things from beyond your understanding, but, even in your sleep, God honors how you have chosen to govern yourself. If you want more dreams and relationship with God during the night, give Him permission to influence you and change you as you sleep. A prayer to give Him authority over your nights, asking Him to change you into His likeness as you sleep, will overrule limitations you may have established in your waking hours.

We sometimes know right away what dreams from God mean. Sometimes the meaning only becomes clear over time. We might have to find someone who has the gift of interpretation. Do not think simplistically about dreams. God uses them in complex ways and may encode several ideas and several time frames into one dream. As with all of His communication to us, documenting what happens will help us focus on the connection we have with Him.

This is a cursory glance at a multidimensional topic, but we want to highlight that, in everything we do, and in every way of relating to God, the Operating System of Jesus quickly opens up empowering union. When we take away the Operating System of Judgment, we take away our judgments about how hearing from God "should" work or how easy or hard it "should" be. We also take away the comparative benchmarking between people; "Do I hear from God more or less than you? Are my visions more or less significant than yours?" All of that noise ceases when we leave the Operating System of Judgment behind. In the quiet of being connected to God, safely held away from the chattering Sanhedrin, all of His communication is more noticeable.

A Healing Word

I had to farewell one of my team members. They had wrecked their knee in a sporting accident and they were returning to their hometown and family for surgery and six months of rehabilitation. They were very sad about the extent of their injuries, and many of us were really sad at their leaving. I am not great at saying goodbye, so I asked God what I should write in the farewell card I had purchased. Immediately, the thought came into my head "Hebrews 12:12." I am not too proud to admit that I had no idea what that verse said so I looked it up and read with complete excitement,

"12. Therefore strengthen the hands which hang down, and the feeble knees;

13. and make straight paths for your feet so that what is lame may not be dislocated but rather healed."

It turned out to be an amazing farewell. Both of us felt so deeply brooded over by God; knowing that He was there in the pain and the process.

Learning To Walk

Following the voice of God in small things will grow us the courage to follow His voice in the weightier issues of life. Living a life of moving with the voice of God is an art form. To do it beautifully requires childlikeness, consecration, great courage, love, and patience. I do not want to make light of its complexity. Neither do I want to dissuade anyone from fully opening up the entire realm of communication as they allow God to grow them into intimate union. Many things feel impossibly difficult, before we learn to do them.

Walking is impossibly complex; a child's body spends one or two years preparing to do something so difficult. Once the preparation is complete, learning to walk happens over a period of weeks, but it is sometimes years before kids can run beautifully with a mature stride. We can delight in the process of learning to move with the living God, knowing that living life from our connection is more than "following the voice." We do not need to be perfectionistic about it. Childlike permission to communicate transitions us from communication into multidimensional union; God in us and us in Him. In that state, communication can become God's signature; the author's initials on the story of our life.

A Learning Experience

Driving to the dog show, my son and I were talking about the steep learning curve we were on. We were disorganized getting ready for the show that morning. My wife laughed and said, "Next time you guys need to get a score better than a 3/10 for your preparation!" She said that before we got lost on the way to the Kennel Club. "Maybe today is going to all be about learning lessons outside the ring?" I suggested to my son.

Things went perfectly in the ring that day. Our pup won best in his class. Later that afternoon, our family was visiting a large shopping center together. As we went up an escalator, my son was telling his brothers how we had suspected the lessons that day were to be learned outside the ring, and how it had turned out to be that way: we took first prize despite our rushed and haphazard morning.

My son turned from his brothers to see a large electronic billboard advertising a movie right in front of where we were talking. The slogan read, "The Battle is Outside the Ring." Excitedly, he drew our attention to God's signature on the small details of our lives. The billboard flashed to a different advertisement.

UNCTION

Unction is an old-fashioned word meaning to move freely, without hesitation, at the leading of the Holy Spirit. It really could be described as being free to enjoy multidimensional union with God. We become more and more confident in moving this way with God through experience. It is part of growing into the "easy yoke" (Matthew 11:30) that Jesus promised us. It happens when we set, not just our communication free, but our whole selves free to speak and move with God.

150

A Story of Healing

I remember very clearly the first time I let myself operate out of "unction" on behalf of another person. I had chosen to become less conscious of what people thought of me so that my perception of their thoughts would not inhibit me. One morning in church, I was worshipping at the back of the sanctuary, and I saw a woman lying down on a beanbag. All the way through worship, I was filled with compassion for her.

The woman approached me after the meeting to tell me how she had been in an accident and had nerve damage throughout her back and down one side of her torso. She was in extreme pain most of the time. I prayed for her out of my compassion, not from my mind, for at least five minutes. I cannot recall what I prayed. I went so deeply into God that I lost awareness of whatever else was going on in the room. I had a sense of angelic activity in the moment, and I am sure I looked strange. To me, it felt like I left my earthly awareness and entered into an awareness only of God.

All of that changed about ten minutes after I left church. I was attacked by self-awareness, doubt, and self-accusation. I remember driving home completely shocked at how I had behaved. I wondered if people were watching me and if I seemed crazy. I was weeping at times during the prayer, and I considered how ridiculous that could have seemed. I even went as far as to speculate that the woman was probably desperate for the prayer time to end. What happened? I had come back from the faith realm, in which my awareness of God was dominant, and, out of habit, started to second guess what I had done. I handed myself over to the Sanhedrin, the demonic voices of condemnation, and they were quick to respond.

The next weekend, I was back at church and the story of that woman's healing was being celebrated. She went to her physical therapist that week, and he told her that the equivalent of eighteen months of "progressive healing" happened in a week.

Theologians use the word 'perichoresis' to describe how God relates to and functions within Himself, a type of multidimensional dancing between the Father, Jesus, and Holy Spirit in perfect union with Themselves. Jesus invited us to join into that union. Our simple obedience will open up our own complex life dance with the Creator who loves us and wants to be our foundational resource under every moment of our lives. The goodness of the destination is beyond what a human mind in the Operating System of Judgment can comprehend. So, we are wooed by God out of that system by a very simple proposal: "Obey me." Childlike obedience opens up a life of God-empowered wonders. If God invited us into it by a full description of its wonder, it would be too good to believe.

Our life in God can quickly become a great feast. Outside of the limits that judgment puts on our minds, we have the eyes to see and the ears to hear. God communicates with us however He wishes to. We get to enjoy Him as He moves through us. You will have dozens of stories of times when you have done things with or for God without consciously knowing you were; perfect moments of His living nature working through you.

> *The tongue that speaks words from God creates life.*

Chapter 12

A NEW EMOTIONAL LANDSCAPE

Transitioning our emotions away from the influence of the Operating System of Judgment and into the living reality of what God is doing, is an important part of establishing union with God. The process can be awkward, and many people experience internal resistance because their emotions have become a trusted "friend," helping them navigate as well as possible without God. Understanding this helps us to put aside, and grow beyond our reservations and take up the opportunity God has given us to be a "new creation" (2 Corinthians 5:17). The full opportunity Jesus bought for us, *"That they also may be one in Us,"* is an opportunity to have our senses, intellect, and emotions directly referenced to the living reality of Father God as He carries out His redemption plans for the planet (John 17:21).

> *God gave humans an emotional life.*

The recalibration of our emotions into the Operating System of Jesus is particularly important. Emotions are extraordinary phenomenon. They are a crossover aspect of being human - a direct bridge between the natural realm and the spirit realm. Emotions are impossible to separate from our psychology but are equally entwined with our physiology. God gave humans an emotional life. Emotions are a valuable part of His design for us. If we live directly from our connection to Him, human emotions bring indefinable depth to our experiencing of God.

As our life transitions into a multidimensional journey of God's living presence, emotions become just one element of a life that is as much art and mystery as it is process.

Emotions are Not Designed For Navigation

Adam and Eve, having chosen to direct themselves without God, were left to harness whatever abilities and resources they could to make their guiding decisions. In the Operating System of Judgment, the highest directing authority a person can access is oneself. This person is the one who has to navigate towards whatever they have decided success is. They are the one who has to minimize risk on that journey. The individual is the governor of all decisions and the one who chooses which of the available resources will be most helpful. People were not designed for this. People were designed to function in close connection to God. Attempting to navigate life without Him is an onerous assignment.

Trying to navigate without God from within the Operating System of Judgment, emotions offer themselves to people as a compelling resource. They are easily judged to be an important navigational tool: They are available; they are powerful, and, because they are often intrinsically related to earthly things, they can easily be assumed to be important indicators of what is unquestionably real. People instinctively engage emotions as a resource to help make decisions. For example, when trying to make a decision, a person draws on their emotions and thinks, "Well, I know I won't be happy if ... so I am going to go with option 'A.'" Additionally, emotions can be used as validators of our choices. Take, for example, a thought like this, "Everyone felt encouraged, so it was the right program to present,"

In the emotional ecosystem created by the Operating System of Judgment, every moment of emotion has a meaning attached to it. The combination of emotion and meaning is usually assumed to be an experience of truth. There is something about the spiritually compelling nature of emotions and the code of meaning we put around them that makes them feel like comprehensive and believable navigation tools. They make us feel connected to truth and we feel like we understand their impact.

Inside the Operating System of Judgment, much time and thought is spent aiming life towards activity and circumstance that will produce the most positive emotion, or working out how to avoid situations and circumstances that cause emotions that are undesirable. In this way, emotions regulate almost all of what a person does, both in the moment and into the future.

Both secular and religious cultures that people establish under the Operating System of Judgment will be grouped around the beliefs and behaviors that validate preferred emotional experiences. For example, people who don't mind sorrow might be able to pray for and serve disenfranchised people for decades. Someone else who can't handle sadness may have to develop a program that brings overt experiences of joy to that kind of group, or choose a completely different kind of work altogether. In this way, our emotional profile can be used by the Operating System of Judgment to provide inputs that "edit out" certain realities that we feel we need to avoid.

Emotions and Decision-Making

Emotions are used on both sides of the decision-making process. Initially, to inform us as part of gathering information needed for a decision; then, to critique the success of the decision after it has been acted upon. When emotions are used in this way to validate our decisions, a dynamic of self-validation gets structured in to our lives. People reach out to God, but when they are caught in this dynamic, they are emotionally predisposed to look for a version of Him that affirms the judgments and assumptions they believe will make them feel the way they most need to feel.

Trusting our emotions as a navigation tool without God's input hurts us. We pay a high price for the practice. If our emotions have executive influence over our decisions, we will not make our decisions in the context of God's best purposes for us. We will make them with an unintentional lock-in to human limitation. As our story plays out, these limits will be expressed. Our trust in ourselves will be undermined over time as we discover how harmful forces that we could not foresee or influence have been able to infiltrate our history.

Much preferable to determining our future by our past, is the process of allowing God to write part of His story through our lives. His story is written around His purposes and backed up by His resources and protection. As He writes a story with us, we will see how much we can trust Him. The process builds our connection with God. Emotions become what they are supposed to be: Special effects that remind us of the genius backstage. We learn not to take them at face value. Emotions are an invitation into a much bigger spirit realm and the opportunity to navigate that space with God.

> *If our emotions have executive influence over our decisions, we will not make our decisions in the context of God's best purposes for us.*

They are not a utilitarian tool to affirm something as static and constricting as human judgment. The relationship between emotions and truth is very malleable and plastic. As time passes, experience will tell us that emotions are a good indicator that something is going on, but will not tell us accurately what that "something" is. The opportunity to live with God is the opportunity to live in direct communion with the One who builds realities. Emotions are whispers on the journey; the fragrance of things beyond our immediate situation to invite us deeper into the landscapes of God.

Emotions of Proximity

Often people are programmed to recoil from the very emotion that proximity to God causes them to feel. Sometimes people feel like crying in the presence of God, a feeling that very closely resembles extreme sadness. Other people might feel exhilaration; God is immense and His living presence can be felt. It is possible for Him to move gently and delicately, but our emotional response to Him can still be very strong. For those who are negatively conditioned around strong emotions, this is a cruel but not uncommon setup. It can cause people to try to shy away from God. It can cause them to reconnect to the apparent safety of the previously whirring machine of judgment that they felt they could control.

People sometimes pull back from the awakening and knowing of God because they don't like the extreme emotions of it; this reality must be processed because it is a residue of the impact of the Operating System of Judgment. It is our mixture of judgment and the creation of realities out of emotional experience. But, God is meeting us and inviting us into His realities. He has to remain faithful to Himself. He has to continue to be the ultimate truth and let our emotions resolve as we recalibrate into Him.

He cannot become a manipulator of us and cause us to have the emotional responses around Him that we are comfortable with. To do so would be God agreeing to become a part of our distorted perception of Him. If we can have the courage to let our emotions do whatever they want to as we learn to encounter the living presence of God, then God will become our soul's infinite anchor. The vulnerability we feel as we transition into knowing Him ultimately becomes a relationship of deep strength.

Emotional Regimes

Sometimes, often for religious reasons, people commit to living under a specific emotional regime. An example of this would be a personal requirement to always be thankful. This decision is rooted in the belief that this behavior or emotion will result in some valued outcome. It is an evidence-based strategy developed out of the Operating System of Judgment. God does not conform to our emotional programs. His living presence will not morph itself to fit our commitment to an emotional strategy. God is always inviting us to grow into something better than we already have. He is who He is and the emotional impact of being near Him will always be an invitation for us to step into His superior reality. If we try to dictate an emotional range, we will be dictating limits to God. Inside the Operating System of Judgment a human is the functional godhead, looking for God to affirm our emotional "truth."

If, for example, we are in circumstances that cause strong negative emotion, it feels "logical" to hope that God will turn the circumstances around in a way that will relieve us of the emotional distress we are under. It is often a cultural norm to hope for emotional relief from God, but it is more effective to know how to access Him, even in emotionally challenging situations, so that we become people who never lose our connection to Him. When we know that we can stay on His track through any kind of situation, we continue to grow into His likeness. Rather than God validating our emotional realities, we grow instead into the reality of His wisdom and abilities. We get to know Him as the God who makes a way in every situation as we become His overcoming sons and daughters.

> *Emotions are an invitation into a bigger spirit realm and the opportunity to navigate that space with God.*

A New Emotional Landscape

In the Operating System of Jesus, we get to swap navigating by human emotions for a simple emotional sensitivity to what God is doing. Outside of judgment and sin, emotions work well. They are part of our ability to *know* and be *known*. Get rid of judgment and its structures and there will be a greater congruence between what you are feeling and what is real to God. It is a great opportunity but one that people are emotionally programmed to avoid. Perhaps that is why God encourages us that, on the other side of the transition, there is rest and peace.

> *Rather than God validating our emotional realities, we grow into the reality of His wisdom and abilities.*

In Matthew 11:28-30 Jesus states, *"Come to Me, all you who labor and are heavy laden, and I will give you rest. Take My yoke upon you and learn from Me, for I am gentle and lowly in heart, and you will find rest for your souls. For My yoke is easy and My burden is light."*

Jesus is not speaking in terms of the emotion of an experience, rather in terms of eternal realities into which we can transition. God understands emotion. He is the creator of our capacity to feel it, but He beckons us into a close relationship with Him so that our emotional life will be lived from the secure place of connection, without the weighty burden of having to navigate our own survival.

If we train our emotions to be consistently referenced to God, our human capacity to feel emotion becomes a very fast and effective way for people to work with God. Emotions will still be part of how we navigate in the Operating System of Jesus, but referenced back to God, we will not be navigating towards our success or survival. Instead, emotions will help us discern His movements in the moment, what He wants to do through us, or they will clue us into His nature, inviting us deeper into friendship. Our emotions become invitations. They are invitations to discover or to understand more of God; to get to know Him better.

The more childlike we can be with God, the more our emotions will get the opportunity to be a fresh and vital part of our connection. The childlikeness takes away the Operating System of Judgment's permission to add layers of asserted meaning onto what we experience. If we can generate a motivation to start to give God "first rights" to our emotional life, we will quickly start to see the power of His light and the benefit of accessing Him as the highest power over all human experience.

Peter's Story

I really hate fighting with my wife. In the early years of our marriage, I realized I actually believed in the conflict as it was happening, and caused a lot of pain with my words. Then, a few days later the whole fight would have seemed unnecessary. In hopes I would stop myself from doing unnecessary damage to my marriage, I made a commitment to God to consult Him at the start of any conflict beginning between us. I promised Him that I would ask Him for His input and listen to whatever He had to say. I have stuck to my commitment and have found God has always had something to teach me about myself, and something for me to do that diffuses the conflict. Not one time has He left me in my pain or helped me to justify my anger. I found that as long as I am prepared to let go of the reasons for my side of the conflict, He always led me from the place of impasse, marked by high emotion, into an understanding that restored my relationship with my wife.

Emotions vs. Truth

Choosing not to assume that our emotions are directly connected to truth gives us the option to break momentarily from our intern conviction. In that space, we can be "poor in spirit" (Matthew 5:3). This is a moment of not knowing. If we can grab that gap and link the moment to God via a simple question, then God Himself can disciple us through the complexity of emotions. "Why do I feel like this?" is a good question to start with. Generally, most people's spirits are so desperate to do a good job navigating with the Operating System of Judgment that they will answer that question for God themselves: *"You are right to feel this unsettled. No one in this corporation appreciates what you bring,"* or some other veiled, but equally self-protecting, justification.

So two more useful questions to ask Holy Spirit would be:

- "How can I access your redemptive life right now as clearly as I can access this emotion?"
- "What can I learn about you and what I am experiencing right now that I have not had the ability to discern before?"

Questions like these will help us to know that we have connected to the God who is above and beyond our understanding rather than our own spirit. Emotion that we allow to be referenced to God will take us from a limited human experience into the vast terrain of a personal journey inside the heart of the infinite God. The transition requires care.

Much of a person's innate emotional repertoire is often formed under the Operating System of Judgment. This means it can be intrinsically reactivated even though someone has broken out of the Operating System of Judgment and the demonic realm no longer has legal access to them. At the moment of reactivation, if thoughts are added back in to justify the old emotional triggers, then a person can quickly stumble back into the old mechanisms. Realizing this, and pulling back out of it quickly, is a powerful way to build new commitment to an emotional life that stays in God.

I spent the evening feeling so sad. The sadness increased, so I went away to spend some time praying. God said to me that a large number of people died, so He was grieving. I stayed with Him in prayer on and off the whole night. The next morning, we all woke to the news that more than fifty people died in a train crash.

Invitations to God's Ways

There are deep aspects to God that we will be invited to explore when emotions are free to come alive to Him. It is possible for our emotional ecosystem to be completely God-referenced. This has direct and immediate benefit to the individual, God, and the people around us. We can fully open up to all that He is without fear of the emotional effect of that fullness, and we can learn to move as He does, because the navigation tool of our emotions will be restored to its proper use – helping us learn to discern God so that we can stay with what He is doing.

As we become less loyal to the emotional codes we were used to, our process of getting to know God accelerates. We develop the habit of filtering all our emotional experiences through God first so what we feel is felt in reference to Him. A person who lives in full connection to God will develop their intellect and thinking in a similar way: All of the aspects of being a human transition into God, so the dominant reality being manifest through our humanity is God.

Katrina's Story

Katrina told me that her Dad was dying. The doctors told her to come to the hospital as soon as possible. When she told me, I remember feeling peace, but also a sense of brightness, almost laughter. It felt so inappropriate, but looking back, I think it was God letting me know that He had no intention of this man dying. That feeling gave me an unusual confidence, so I suggested we pray. We thanked God that Katrina's Dad was to live and not die. Not only did he not die, but he left the hospital, apparently completely well, that very same day.

God Training our Emotions

Letting God train our emotions into Him will give us opportunity to see how good and how powerfully loving He is. But, for many, a lifetime under the condemning commentary of the Operating System of Judgment will have them emotionally conditioned to be extremely wary of God and wired against trusting Him with something as deeply personal as our emotions. The Operating System of Judgment conditions people to be afraid of forces more powerful than one's self. The fear is always that we could be overtaken, dominated, or manipulated. This creates an instinct to keep away from an unknown and all-powerful being, even if it is God and He is the source of all that is good. People become predisposed to resist experiencing the love of God.

Let's take a look at the God who wants us close. Let's take this opportunity to let Him show us who He really is, and break through any preconceptions we allow to protect ourselves:

Even as Jesus prepared for the ordeal of the crucifixion, He kept His disciples close, asking them to keep watch over Him as He agonized in prayer with His Father (Matthew 26). The God-man, who was about to bring complete redemption to the world, wanted His friends to be with Him as He approached the greatest imaginable trial. It is a vivid picture of the value for humans God has as He prepared to reconnect mankind with Himself.

Anyone who has known separation from someone they love desperately can understand the agony of love. We are made in God's image. We can all feel at least a shadow of God's longing by imagining or experiencing that pain. But the pain of human separation is only a taste of the longing in the heart of God for connection to people who were born to experience "*abundant life*" through their union with Him (John 10:10). It is this longing for full connection with mankind that has authored every line of each one of God's redemption stories.

The Operating System of Judgment tries to cancel out the validity of longing, but it cannot obliterate the deep yearning inside people. It will tell us how we should "reasonably" satisfy our appetites, but it will bombard people with a lifetime of well-crafted strategy to prevent them from having their deepest longing fulfilled in communion with the One who is the origin of all goodness. We are created to be like God, and we are designed to only find fulfillment in union with Him.

God's Love for His People

The sum total of all of the emotion in the world cannot equal the immense emotional power that compelled the heart of God to re-establish union with mankind. In Numbers 14:11, the God of the universe confesses to His friend, Moses, how frustrated He is by His apparent inability to win the affection of the people He so desperately cares for (the Israelites). "*Then the Lord said to Moses, 'How long will these people reject me? And how long will they not believe Me, with all the signs which I have performed among them?'*" The Old Testament is full of proclamations of God's desire for these children of Abraham's promise. In Deuteronomy 10:15, Moses said: "*The Lord delighted only in your fathers, to love them; and He chose their descendants after them, you above all peoples, as it is this day.*"

There is nothing "rational" about God's desperate love for the Israelites. They were His original family on the planet, the family through whom God chose to make Himself known. Deuteronomy 7:7 records that love alone is the reason God was so stuck on these people, "*The LORD did not set His love on you nor choose you because you were more in number than any other people, for you were the least of all peoples.*"

God's love constantly provoked Him to look for ways to bless these people. In Deuteronomy 7:13, Moses says: "And He will love you and bless you and multiply you; He will also bless the fruit of your womb and the fruit of your land, your grain and your new wine and your oil, the increase of your cattle and the offspring of your flock, in the land of which He swore to your fathers to give you."

Many of God's friends were indeed extremely blessed:

•Abraham was one of the wealthiest people of his time and, from one son late in life, his descendants became a nation.

•Joseph rose to a place of honor, second only to the king of Egypt.

•David's success as a warrior king made a mighty nation of Israel.

•Solomon was known throughout the world, not only for riches, but also for wisdom.

God's ability to love His people by blessing them was constantly hindered as they persistently chose to direct their lives away from Him. It hurt God. The separation caused God great distress. The Old Testament is full of descriptions of the longing of God over a separation that He cannot bear.

Jeremiah 2:2: *"Go and cry in the hearing of Jerusalem, saying, 'Thus says the LORD: 'I remember you, The kindness of your youth, the love of your betrothal, when you pursued me in the wilderness.'"* Song of Songs 3.1: *"By night on my bed I sought the one I love; I sought him but I did not find him."* And Song of Songs 5:8: *"I charge you, O daughters of Jerusalem, if you find my beloved, that you tell him that I am lovesick."*

The descriptions of God's longing for the restoration of union with His people only increase as history approaches the arrival of the Messiah. In Isaiah 42:14b, the Lord says: *"Now I will cry like a woman in labor, I will pant and gasp at once."* And Chapter 43:1c, *"I have called you by your name. You are mine."* Then, in verses 3b-4a, *"I gave Egypt for your ransom, Ethiopia and Seba in your place. Since you were precious in My sight, you have been honored, and I have loved you."*

The prophets continue with God's apparent obsession: His longing for, His planning for, and His delivery of, restoration: Isaiah 44:21c-22: *"Oh Israel, You will not be forgotten by me! I have blotted out, like a thick cloud, your transgressions, and like a cloud, your sins. Return to Me, for I have redeemed you."* Finally, if we were not yet convinced, Isaiah 49: 15-16a states:

"Can a woman forget her nursing child, And not have compassion on the son of her womb? Surely they may forget, but I will not forget you. See I have inscribed you on the palms of My hands."

For thousands of years in the Old Testament, God pressed on through His frustrations, waiting for the day when He would present Jesus to the world. After Jesus, the records and descriptions of this longing cease. Why? Because Jesus made a way for God to have what He has always wanted - intimate connection to humans.

The Operating System of Judgment, while still an option, is no longer the only option. The operating system that allows people to live from their connection to God is now in place. Jesus is the incarnation of God's heart towards the planet and God's proposal to overcome the separation for all time. Titus 3:4 states: *"But when the kindness and the love of God our savior toward man appeared..."*

The record of God's desire for reconnection to mankind diminishes once we reach the New Testament. After the death of Jesus, that longing in God is now satisfied by every individual who opens up their heart to know God as He is. We develop a connection with God that is free, powerful, and effective. Rather than being people who try to love, we become people who manifest God without specifically trying. Circumstances change around people who allow every part of them to teach them about God and deliver Him to the planet around them.

167

A World in Need of Love

The planet has seen what it looks like when theology is exalted above human experience and people are told that their emotions have to come into line with theology. It has seen what it looks like when people switch themselves off, supposedly becoming demonstrations of sacrificial love, but really they become annihilated automatons for a set of beliefs representing a demanding idea of the divine. Unwilling to continue to model the emotional annihilation in the name of Jesus, people have tried to elevate the individual, our desires, needs, and longings. This leads to reinventing theology to try to create a kinder experience; a self-satisfying redesign of the décor in the prison system created by human judgment.

> *There is no point pretending that a particular inflection of Christianity will satisfy our emotional needs or be the answer to the emotional needs of humankind.*

But the world has grown able to see just how malleable the human "realities" of our emotions can be. Those who study human behavior show us that most of our thinking and emotions are able to be adjusted to maintain whatever effect we decide is most desired by us or those around us; often, this is a process with great emotional cost which we will not discover until much later.

In response to the planet's genuine need for God, we have tried to present happier Christians and a more appealing gospel, but trying to evolve our theology to fit our times belies a structural issue: a lack of integrity. History tells us that it is equally repulsive to continue with emotional suppression in the name of God. There is no point pretending that a particular inflection of Christianity will satisfy our emotional needs or be the answer to the emotional needs of humankind. Self-governed religious practitioners have always been induced by the spirit realm into hidden and corrupt behaviors that leave a legacy of pain to tell the world how unable they were to be emotionally satisfied by life under a religious code.

The planet will become a living picture of God's redemptive power when the emotional ecosystems of individuals and nations are recalibrated into God. God will be experienced in real time and people will be anchored into the One who is eternal and infinite. If we can allow God to reveal Himself to us as He actually is, we will discover we can trust Him. We can grow a loyalty to Him because we are safe. Then, our emotions can all grow to be referenced through Him.

What He has for us will come alive. The self-protective emotional realities of the Operating System of Judgment will no longer seem relevant to us. We get to feel His immediate, active presence and situations around us get to see what God looks like as He fathers His kids and ministers to His expectant planet.

> *If we can allow God to reveal Himself to us as He actually is, we will discover we can trust Him. We can grow a loyalty to Him because we are safe.*

Chapter 13

CASTING FRESH LIGHT ON THE BIBLE
How does God Speak Through His Written Word?

The *Bible* is the best-selling book of all time. It has a long and colorful history of use, abuse, devotion, and disdain. As sacred Scripture, it is a God-breathed gift to help us find our way to relationship with Him. As a book, it has been used to promote one idea or another, justify actions, and lend authority to different causes. The *Bible* is not immune from being used to inflict harm. When Satan tempted Jesus in the wilderness, His weapon of choice was Scripture. Matthew 4: 5-6:

> "*Then the devil took Him up into the holy city, set Him on the pinnacle of the temple, and said to Him, "If you are the Son of God, throw Yourself down. For it is written: 'He shall give His angels charge over you,' and, 'In (their) hands they shall bear you up, lest you dash your foot against a stone.'"*

The devil's challenge to Jesus was an attempt to persuade Him to operate away from His connection to God. Satan was trying to do to Jesus what He had successfully done to Eve thousands of years before. This time, Satan used Scripture to borrow authority from God for his propositions. His intention was to take Jesus off His assignment. Satan's use of Scripture is a clear demonstration that evil will not hesitate to use Scripture for harm, so it is no surprise that an operating system marked by separation from God will skew our application of the *Bible* in ways that harm our connection to Him.

Mental Assent

A range of scholarly methods have evolved to help understand, interpret, and guide application of the *Bible* to our lives. While these methods can be useful, it is important that academic processes are not permitted to lock up our minds as we study. God, and each person He indwells, must be free to come alive to each other as that person searches within God-breathed Scripture.

The *Bible*, and the body of learning and tradition associated with it, is a corporate treasure of the body of Christ. We must adopt a way of studying it that causes us to have and grow in intimate relationship with the resurrected Jesus. We must let the *Bible* lead us to move with Holy Spirit so we become deeply-connected friends of God who think, do, and say exactly what Father God is doing. Study of Scripture needs to propel us towards a life of being grafted into the vine.

When we dethrone the judge in our minds, the *Bible* takes on fresh new life. We are no longer limited to our rational and intellectual constructs. Holy Spirit is free to open up body, mind, and spirit connection between us, the written Scriptures, and Father God. Academic and intellectual traditions become honored points of consideration and provide options and tools to help us. The *Bible* becomes a discovery book about our Father God and our friend Jesus, who is closer to us than a brother. We get to discover aspects of our heavenly Father and how we can come fully alive in Him.

> *An operating system marked by separation from God will apply the Bible in ways that harm our connection to Him.*

The Pharisees had a very strong relationship with the written Word of God, but the strength of their relationship with Scripture did not result in being able to recognize Jesus or the life He offered them. In John 5:38-40, Jesus said:

> *"But you do not have His word abiding in you, because whom He sent, Him you do not believe. You search the Scriptures, for in them you think you have eternal life; and these are they which testify of Me. But you are not willing to come to Me that you may have life."*

Imprisoned by Rules

It is entirely possible for people today to put wholehearted faith in the study of Scripture and unintentionally end up in the same position as the Pharisees. Jesus said they knew Scripture but did not come to Him to have life. We can know Scripture and know about Jesus, but not know Him personally even though He is completely available to us.

Jesus did not tell the Pharisees how to appropriately "know" Scripture. He didn't tell them what was wrong with their judgments and assumptions, and how to correct their understanding to "get it right." He could not set captives free by joining them in the very practice causing imprisonment. He can not join the captives in "redecorating the prison." We may feel empowered when we make a change, but no "tweaking" will make a deadly operating system become life-giving. When someone is in jail, they are in jail.

Celebrating God as He is recorded in the Bible, but at the same time expecting less from Him today, uses the Bible as God-themed entertainment while we live in a prison of our own assumptions. It is sad to use the Bible to enrich life in the jail. If you are drawing heavily for nourishment on the details of God you find in someone else's life, or in some other time period, you can be confident that there is much more available for you. Our living connection with God is the power that frees us from the custodial way of life. Regularly redecorating the cells of our jail with new ways to be right or feel purposeful will not do. A preoccupation with "appropriately" interpreting Scripture may be showing us that we have still not "come to Jesus." In John 5:40, Jesus expects that "coming to Him" will produce life.

Chapter 14

BRIEF OVERVIEW OF THE BIBLE:
From an Operating Systems Perspective

The Old Testament begins with the story of God, His planet, and the people He created to share it with Him. We have already looked in detail at what happened in the Garden of Eden and mankind's entry into the Operating System of Judgment. Adam and Eve's decision to activate themselves in the Operating System of Judgment meant that all people on earth came under "natural law" and entered into a relationship with limitation and sin. Despite this decision, thousands of years of history demonstrate the heart of God preserving a tribe of His chosen people – the Israelites. They were His representatives from the original DNA He released on the planet. For God, it was clearly important that His redemption plan would come to the earth through them; His chosen people to whom He had pledged His love.

God's people, the Israelites, lived under the Operating System of Judgment and showed God over and over again how they wanted to navigate out of their own strength. Nonetheless, God brooded over them like an involved parent, taking every opportunity to keep them close and protect them from harm. Because mankind opted for the Operating System of Judgment, they became vulnerable to forces beyond their understanding. To protect them from harm, God, in His infinite understanding, offered them a code of limits called "The Law."

The Legal Code

This legal code served two purposes. Firstly, it provided protective boundaries for behavior. Because they were prescribed by a perfect and loving God, they were wise and benevolent boundaries. Secondly, the legal code included ways to process the consequences of sin out of their lives, leaving them with a measure of holiness so that they could be close to God and God could stay close to them. God needed a way to "neutralize" or "atone for" the effect of the sin or evil; He needed a way to "cleanse" evil off His people.

It was important to God that He could keep pulling His people away from the worst of conditions that the Operating System of Judgment could lead them into. Until Jesus came and released the whole planet from its entanglement with the Operating System of Judgment, God organized for these effects to be routinely processed away. Some of the Israelites, most usually His priests, were genuinely able to come into contact with Him even though the Operating System of Judgment gave most of the population very little access to Him. This is the reason for the use of sacrifices.

Although the Law made some access to God available, it was neither the measure of union Jesus later asked for.

If sin or evil were able to leave its residue on the people, this increasing evil legacy would have repelled itself from God's goodness and taken the people with it. Legally displacing the residue of judgment and sin onto a sacrificial animal meant the sacrificial animal could be separated out from God (ultimately death), allowing the people to remain closer. "The Law" laid out the procedures whereby the whole community could be regularly divested of these burdens and God could stay close.

Although the Law made some access to God available, it was neither the measure of union Jesus later asked for, nor did it satisfy the longing of Father God. At times, God would appear as a pillar of cloud or fire to lead them; at other times, His presence rested in or on a sacred object. The Ark of the Covenant was kept in either the tabernacle or the temple as a representation of the Presence of God, but there was nothing like the "indwelling" or full connection that is available to mankind now.

God was loosely managing people who were made in His image but living out their godlikeness without Him. God's access to the people He loved was constrained by the limits Eve empowered - the human capacity to direct itself through judgment. Despite that, some individuals developed great friendships with God, most notably, Moses and David. As a whole, the history of Israel as a people group was one of God's tending, their periodic desire for connection, and a demonstration over the centuries of their systemic inability to grow into intimate relationship with God. Still God insisted that He could bring about a global love story through the harsh history of life under a legal code.

God Authors His Story

God maintained a family line, a bloodline of people He called to be close to Him. Abraham and Sarah struggled to believe and set about organizing for their inheritance to be passed on through the child of a maid because it seemed they were too old to have the child God promised them. In Genesis 17, God starts to talk to Abraham about what He wants to do and Abraham pleads with God, "*Oh, that Ishmael might live before You!*" (Genesis 17:18). It is a powerful moment when God's friend, Abraham, is disarmingly real with God, pleading with God to accept a plan that he and Sarah cooked up in their unbelief. But God is true to Himself and says that He wants to achieve His bloodline through His choice, and insists Sarah will bear a child. This promise is still given even though she is so old that physically it is now "impossible."

The legal code of life under the law may appear coercive and restrictive to modern people. But God gave His people limits inspired and protected by His infinite wisdom and designed to lead them toward an eternal outcome driven by love. The only other reality in the Operating System of Judgment is vulnerability under the limits we create through our own judgment and finite understanding.

If the code of the Old Testament law is reviewed from inside of the Operating System of Judgment it will always be interpreted with a bias toward the possibility of fear, threats, and punishment. Less powerful beings (people) in the Operating System of Judgment are forced to use themselves to navigate around the more powerful being (God). People will always be on alert to the threat the more powerful being could represent (without a sure trust in the more powerful being's benevolence). Thus, it is hard to read Scripture written by people under that operating system without picking up on their bias. They were scared.

Misunderstanding God

God's burning desire for connection with His people is constantly misperceived under the Operating System of Judgment. This operating system distorts how the human mind functions. From the time the operating system is activated in a person, perception is skewed towards judgment, which invites fear, intimidation, and expectation of punishment. In Numbers 14:11, God asks, *"How long will these people reject me? And how long will they not believe Me, with all the signs which I have performed among them?"* As long as people are inside a judgment operating system, their perception of God is not accurate. No matter how much He blessed them, they were never free from their corrupted perception.

Likewise for us, if we read the *Bible* through the lens of the Operating System of Judgment, the weightiness of the *Bible's* impact on us will not be the life-giving power of Jesus.

Rather, it will be fear, intimidation, discouragement, and despair, for ourselves, as well as unbelievers. The Operating System of Judgment skews spiritual inputs from any source toward condemnation and incarceration or defensive over-estimation of self.

For thousands of years, human civilization, founded on the Operating System of Judgment, provided complex and convincing demonstrations of the futility of building a civilization on human limitation. As the Book of Ecclesiastes notes, without connection to the life of God through Jesus, there is *"nothing new under the sun"* (Ecclesiastes 1:9). As the centuries passed, and the culture of the Israelites grew more complex, the prescriptions from God about how to keep people safe from the entanglements of the culture and the harm of sin grew more and more detailed.

Relentless God

God remained committed to His original idea for planet Earth. He is a good Father, and He was planning our return to childlike connection. This place has all people in intimate relationship with Him and is the extension of His dominion through all people everywhere. Jesus came to model intimate relationship with the Father, to train people for it, pay the price for it, and ensure that it was established. He ushered in an era in which God was not limited to our "judgment-oriented" perceptions anymore. Jesus was willing to pay a very high price to restore our opportunity to access Father God's loving mercy.

The Old Covenant, when God's commitment to the Israelites was expressed through a legal code and sacrificial cleansing, came to an end with the final sacrifice of God's own Son, Jesus, on the Cross. In His resurrection life, Jesus ascended to Heaven and sent Holy Spirit to empower the New Covenant, the eternal opportunity for all people to come into union with God.

In Jesus, we see the reintroduction of righteousness to the world. Not righteousness under the Law, but a living expression of righteousness, God in human form. The four gospel accounts tell the story of Jesus' life, including clear details of things He said. Jesus' constant choice to stay in connection to the Father is well documented. He maintained a complete freedom from entanglement with the Operating System of Judgment. At the end of His earthly life, Jesus gave Himself to the power of judgment and became the price paid to absorb the full cost of evil on planet Earth.

What follows the New Testament gospels is a documentary of the great reintroduction of God to the planet after Jesus' death and resurrection. God no longer has to hold back. He pours Himself out generously as people make their lives available to Him. In Acts, Romans, 1 and 2 Corinthians, and all the way through to Jude, we read about people learning to live out, and occasional attempts to codify, the new "way" of living with God. Humans could live from a connection to God in a way never seen before. God was truly "Emmanuel" (which means *God with us)* (Isaiah 7:8), the New Testament reality of God who is making Himself at home in people (John 14:23).

Parts of the New Testament are documentary accounts of the lives of people and communities as they transition into this new way of living with God. Other parts are revelatory writings, showing the nature of God and describing our new opportunity to "know" Him intimately (the exploration of our adoption into God in Romans 8). Other parts of the New Testament document times when instruction was given, often in the form of advice given to communities and churches in the process of transitioning into the new way.

After the four gospels, the New Testament documents people and communities discovering their access to the living God. There are accounts of their minds expanding as they caught glimpses of who He is and His nature of love. Jesus' ministry came at a high point of Pharisaic culture and the dominant expression of life at that time was *not* love. Some of the most famous lines of prose are from the revelatory writings of these new Christians.

Paul's System Upgrade

In what is commonly referred to as the "Love Chapter" from 1 Corinthians, written by the Apostle Paul, God's nature of love is chronicled, *"And now abide faith, hope, love, these three; but the greatest of these is love"* (1 Corinthians 13:13). This is one of many accounts by Paul of the love of God. Some of the most inspiring discoveries of new life with the Holy Spirit are documented in the writings by, and about, the Apostle Paul. His letters to several new churches show how these communities grappled with the transition from life without God to life indwelt by God. So much love and hope was released, but in what we read we can still hear the influence of the Operating System of Judgment.

The Apostle Paul was originally a Pharisee. In fact, he described himself as a "Pharisee of Pharisees" (Acts 23:6). His passion as a Pharisee involved bringing to justice people who were doing the "wrong" thing. Early Christians fell into this category. God chose to stop Paul with a powerful supernatural encounter causing the history of this man to be radically changed. His encounter with God "dialed him in" to the Holy Spirit giving him an extraordinary ability to speak and act out of unction with God.

Paul was thrust into leadership of a rapidly expanding Christian community immediately after his dramatic conversion. He was called on to lead large numbers of people at the same time as he was himself still learning the Operating System of Jesus. Till now, those communities he led only knew a culture with a "codebook" (a set of rules and prescribed behaviors). They would have expected their leaders to tell them what to do. Those being led by Paul would only have experienced leadership based on the Operating System of Judgment. What is more, many of the communities he visited or was teaching, had never witnessed Jesus, nor had they ever seen people living out of a direct connection to God. They were used to the old way of doing things, and there would have been enormous pressure on Paul to keep using some of the old form.

Groups who are used to being led from the Operating System of Judgment typically have leaders who are "right" and followers who are dependent on leaders for direction. The new converts in Paul's day, were familiar with compliance. And Paul, as a Pharisee, would have naturally been familiar with giving instruction. As he transitioned from the Operating System of Judgment into a life of knowing God, traces of the old system were working their way out. Being able to learn from Paul's transition process is valuable and informative for us today. Paul's writing is, in part, profound revelation on the nature of love, the nature of grace, and the invitation to know God but, at times, Paul still operated out of the more familiar way that Jesus never turned to, prescribing the "right way" to live out the details of a Christian life.

In 1 Corinthians 5, Paul writes to the Corinthian church to help them deal with a serious moral error in their congregation. He is faced with a situation where a man slept with his own mother. Paul writes a very stern letter: *"For I indeed, as absent in body but present in spirit, have already judged (as though I were present) him who has so done this deed."* His advice follows in verse 4: *"In the name of our Lord Jesus Christ .... deliver such a one to Satan for the destruction of the flesh, that his spirit may be saved in the day of the Lord Jesus"* (1 Corinthians 5:4,5).

Nothing in Paul's response to this situation has anything in common with how Jesus treated people, no matter how serious their sin. The only account in the gospels of any of Jesus' people judging and proposing aggressive action is the story in Luke 9:54 when the disciples asked if Jesus would like them to call down fire on the Samaritan village. Jesus responded: *"You do not know what manner of spirit you are of"* (Luke 9:55).

In 2 Corinthians, Paul commences damage control. He asks the church to now call the man, whom he had judged, back into the body and to treat him with love. In 2 Corinthians 2:8, Paul says *"Therefore I urge you to reaffirm [your] love to him."* Paul seemed to realize the man was isolated and made vulnerable because of his advice and was now at risk. He encourages them to bring him back into community. Paul responds to the damage that has occurred because of his earlier prescription by asserting that his earlier instruction also had a hidden value; it was a test to see if the Corinthians were implicitly obedient to him.

"For to this end I also wrote, that I might put you to the test, whether you are obedient in all things" (2 Corinthians 2:9).

> **Jesus was willing to pay a very high price to restore our opportunity to access Father God's loving mercy.**

Mistakes Happen

Making mistakes is a simple part of being human, but since the Operating System of Judgment is compliance-based, it causes the making of mistakes to be a painful experience. To the spiritual powers that torment people (what Jesus calls the "Sanhedrin" or the "officer"), mistakes legitimize a whole lot of accusation and torment. These spiritual powers conspire to make mistake-making as complex and painful as possible. They keep us alive to condemnation so that our history of mistakes stains our whole future. This further drives people into desperation not to make mistakes; it drives us to always say and do the "right" thing.

Could it be that Paul's background as a Pharisee, a professional practitioner of the Operating System of Judgment, was still making it hard for him to process through simple errors? Could it be that he still had quick access to the pain of making mistakes and some access to the torment of condemnation? When people live in intimacy with God they learn how grace overcomes the power and effect of our mistakes. We can apologize for our errors, be forgiven and move on. For some people, this will be a transition that takes time. Often our emotional responses to condemnation will have to be "unlearned," but the opportunity for mistake making to be a simple part of being human exists for everyone.

Paul truly had a powerful heart-knowledge that grace offered us freedom from the Law (the Operating System of Judgment), freedom from sin, and a connection to the transforming, redemptive power of God. We get to read how that actualized in his leadership in the documentary of his story. He wrote with urgency, wanting to persuade all people everywhere to take the opportunity grace opened up for mankind. Paul found an expression for the completely transformational experience that involved a new mind, a new heart, and new behavior. Paul coined the phrase *"putting on the new man"* (Colossians 3.10). His reference to "the old man" refers to an individual who hasn't yet transitioned away from sin and judgment and into righteousness. Paul's deep desire for believers was that each of us would be a *"new man."*

In his enthusiasm for people to get on with the job and live together successfully in the new way, Paul makes some recommendations that need consideration or interpretation. In 1 Corinthians 11:31, he goes as far as saying that *"If we would judge ourselves, we would not be judged."* Perhaps Paul logically assumed that if we would all hold ourselves accountable for everything we do, problems would resolve quickly. Unfortunately, his suggestion is exactly what Pharisees already did and it required every person to put themselves back under the burden of judgment, albeit with good and selfless intentions. Such teaching deviates far from the practices and teaching of Jesus.

> *When people live in intimacy with God they learn how grace overcomes the power and effect of our mistakes.*

Jesus Restores Relationship

Jesus died for us so that we could live in God's mercy. Jesus invites us to consider how we want to judge people, influencing our choice with a clear statement that "*I judge no one*"(John 8:15). This statement is very different from the lifestyle of the Pharisees; the ones constantly judging and assessing themselves against the standards they created. In the Operating System of Jesus, we live in the clear light of God. In that place, sin is seen for what it is, and mistakes are mistakes. The living words and actions of God are free to flow through us so that God can be seen as He is.

Jesus opened up new territory as He confounded the understanding people built out of judgment. Jesus' new territory opens up through relationship. This territory is supposed to become a life lived out of connection with God. The Apostle Paul was transitioning into God as he did so. We are invited to do the same. There were times on the journey when Paul was prescriptive in detailed ways that Jesus is not. It is understandable that people who are born and raised under the Operating System of Judgment may instinctively try to prescribe aspects of life in God that cannot actually happen by prescribing behaviors.

Evil is always looking for ways to reinstate the demonic chorus of critical and accusing voices.

The Operating System of Judgment always presents us with invitations to bring a living relationship with God back in under a prescriptive code. Self-judgment, as Paul suggests in 1 Corinthians 11:31 links us back into the Operating System of Judgment, creating a barrier to intimacy with God. Evil is always looking for ways to reinstate the demonic chorus of critical and accusing voices- the Sanhedrin. Always, the code is developed out of the assessment, review, and judgment-based recommendations of a person, rather than God. Jesus did very little prescribing but invites us instead into a process that transfuses His nature into us as we learn to live and move in intimacy with Him. The Operating System of Jesus gives God maximum access to shape us into the "new person" He had in mind when He conceived of us.

Paul's Transition

Is it possible that we were supposed to read Paul's writings and see them as a story of a leader, communities, and the known world in transition into the infinite possibilities of life with the God who became one with us? What would happen if Paul's exploration of love and explorations of grace inspired future generations of leaders into even greater discoveries of what is possible when we walk with God and become His friends?

When people read the writings of Paul with a commitment to the Operating System of Judgment they are trying to filter truth into an operating system that exists to minimize the power of truth. In that context, truth arrives distorted, perverted, or lifeless.

People have been partnering with the Operating System of Judgment since the very earliest centuries of the Christian church. The early church devoted great time and resources to this practice much like the church does today. Church leaders have always been pressured to answer to accusations and charges made against them by collecting evidence, reviewing practices, and formulating policy that clarifies beliefs and prescribes preferred behaviors. Jesus was constantly invited into this process by the Pharisees, but He never joined in as they hoped He might. Undaunted by Jesus' complete avoidance of the practice, or perhaps not knowing how to make sense of Jesus apparent inaction, Christians have continued representing God to the planet this way.

The protestant reformation was a huge push against what was perceived as corruption in the church. How did people respond to that corruption? People encoded the "correct thing." Leaders told their people how to "get it right." Unsurprisingly, as the church got more and more "correct" with greater definition of its doctrines, it grew less and less able to demonstrate the measure of connection with God the planet wants, needs, and is supposed to be given. The church became progressively less able to display that God is with us.

The Zeal of God

But losing the connection with the planet God died to achieve is not palatable to God. The prophet Isaiah foretold a great planetary breakout, when all systems of captivity will be unable to hold back their hostages. He is describing the effect of Jesus in Isaiah 45:1-

> *"Thus says the LORD to His anointed, To Cyrus, whose right hand I have held—To subdue nations before him And loose the armor of kings, To open before him the double doors, So that the gates will not be shut:*
>
> *'I will go before you*
> *And make the crooked places straight;*
> *I will break in pieces the gates of bronze*
> *And cut the bars of iron.*
> *I will give you the treasures of darkness*
> *And hidden riches of secret places,*
> *That you may know that I, the LORD,*
> *Who call you by your name,*
> *Am the God of Israel.'"*

In verse 9, God reminds us that none of this will happen out of our good ideas or out of us telling Him what to do, reminding us that He is the potter and we are the clay (Isaiah 45:9). God knows what He is doing. He has been in the jailbreak business a long time. If we break free from agreement with the Operating System of Judgment that drags everything into lockdown, we will actually be able to participate in God's plans for global emancipation.

Chapter 15

THE RICH YOUNG RULER

In the famous story of the Rich Young Ruler, Jesus' devotion and persistence in laying the groundwork for a person to break free into the reality of knowing God is displayed. The story can be viewed from the perspective of both operating systems, and when doing so a different interpretation is present. This is a powerful story:

> Mark 10:17-23:
>
> *Now as He was going out on the road, one came running, knelt before Him, and asked Him, "Good Teacher, what shall I do that I may inherit eternal life?"*
>
> *So Jesus said to him, "Why do you call Me good? No one [is] good but One, [that is], God.*
>
> *"You know the commandments: 'Do not commit adultery,' 'Do not murder,' 'Do not steal,' 'Do not bear false witness,' 'Do not defraud,' 'Honor your father and your mother.'"*
>
> *And he answered and said to Him, "Teacher, all these things I have kept from my youth."*
>
> *Then Jesus, looking at him, loved him, and said to him, "One thing you lack: Go your way, sell whatever you have and give to the poor, and you will have treasure in heaven; and come, take up the cross, and follow Me."*
>
> *But he was sad at this word, and went away sorrowful, for he had great possessions.*

Then Jesus looked around and said to His disciples, "How hard it is for those who have riches to enter the kingdom of God!"

And they were greatly astonished, saying among themselves, "Who then can be saved?"

But Jesus looked at them and said, "With men [it is] impossible, but not with God; for with God all things are possible."

By standing outside of all constraint applied to our thinking by the Operating System of Judgment, the reader is free to understand Jesus' words and to see His heart for the Rich Young Ruler.

In the story, this young man runs enthusiastically up to Jesus, kneels on the ground and says *"Good Teacher, what must I do to inherit eternal life?"* He refers to Jesus as an anointed and noble teacher, using an expression reserved for God. This is a standout moment in all of the stories of Jesus' life. The man had a revelation, or spirit recognition of Jesus' divinity. The man could, however, now be judged to be a blasphemer under Jewish law. The penalty for blasphemy was severe. People were watching this conversation. One move toward Jesus and any number of Pharisees could argue for the Rich Young Ruler to be put to death.

Jesus grabbed this moment of recognition by offering the rich ruler a question; *"Why do you say I am good?"* This was Jesus offering the man an opportunity to overt and activate the recognition that he already had in his spirit, the revelation that Jesus is God. But Jesus was not looking for the man to recognize Him for Jesus' own satisfaction. He was looking for the man to connect to God and pull himself out of the Operating System of Judgment. To have the Rich Young Ruler replace his current "godhead" with a new connection to the living God, Jesus had to present the man with a choice. He had to present both operating systems to the man, back to back, and have the man make his choice. Jesus gave Him two options. He was allowing the rich ruler's spirit to choose which way it wanted to go: he could choose the new spark of recognition of Jesus' divinity or the conviction of his own success under the law.

Presented with Freedom

The decision the man made in that moment had to be a true reflection of himself and not a response to external pressure from a powerful leader (Jesus). Jesus listed these options for the man:

RICH RULER'S OPTION ONE: Pursue connection with Jesus' divinity (Mark 10:18).

"Why do you call Me good?" No one is good but God alone.

RICH RULER'S OPTION TWO: Continue with a history of success under the Operating System of Judgment. (Mark 10:19)

"You know the commandments: 'Do not commit adultery,' 'Do not murder,' 'Do not steal,' 'Do not bear false witness, ...'"

Jesus gives the Rich Young Ruler a powerful choice and uses language to bias the situation towards the man's freedom. He presents the option to recognize Jesus' deity as a question, and offers this question first. The second option, representing the way of "success" under the Operating System of Judgment, is mentioned by Jesus as a simple statement, not connected to any question so that the rich ruler can more easily move past it.

The Rich Young Ruler, however, knows his security in the Operating System of Judgment. Jesus looks at the Rich Ruler, waiting for a response. The Rich Ruler looks at Jesus. Jesus has never been recognized as God publicly in this way before. The passage records Jesus looking at him and loving him.

Choosing Judgment

The Rich Young Ruler's courage lets him down. He responds to Jesus' statement by choosing option two. He defaults to the system that has positioned him well, the Operating System of Judgment. He tells Jesus how he has kept the whole law. The opportunity Jesus gives him to throw his heart behind his conviction that Jesus is God, gets passed over, for now.

It appears that the Rich Ruler is hearing conflicting voices inside his own mind. Just a few short minutes before, he is seriously enthused about coming to Jesus and calling Him God. Perhaps he is now listening to demonic voices urging, "Don't do anything crazy! You might get stoned to death if you say this man is God." or "You have already done a great job at living a respectable life. Just impress Jesus with what you have already done."

Matthew 5:25 tells us the end destination of the Operating System of Judgment is being "in jail" or "under guard." The guards are a demonic force that can speak words and thoughts. If they recognize a person making a break for freedom they will do anything in their power to counsel the prisoner back into peaceful agreement with their incarceration. Jesus does not tell us about the internal conversation the man is having with himself. Jesus did not generally go head to head with evil, so He did not debate with the demonic "Sanhedrin."

A Second Chance

Jesus makes available a second strategy for the man's jailbreak. The young man had already made it clear that he wanted to be free to follow Jesus. He was seeking eternal life and, from the outset, he was certain that Jesus was something extraordinary; deserving of the recognition reserved for God. Jesus set out to secure a heart connection and persisted to try to achieve it.

The first move from Jesus was to provoke the man's heart to courage since the Rich Ruler was already under conviction of Jesus' identity. If that spark of conviction could have been fanned into flame and displaced the man's intellectual jail (the Operating System of Judgment), the Rich Ruler would have been free. But when a person is accustomed to making decisions under the Operating System of Judgment, it is hard for them to let a "knowing" in their spirit come alive. The young man's "knowing" that Jesus was God was undermined by his internal council.

So Jesus proposes the next option, which looks like a mechanical strategy to stack the odds away from the appeal of the Operating System of Judgment. It is the instruction to sell all his possessions, take up the cross and follow Jesus.

Remember that the Rich Ruler was apparently "successful." The godhead of his own mind rewarded him with material wealth. When someone has achieved "success" under the Operating System of Judgment, trophies such as wealth reinforce the perception of value of that system. Many factors worked against the Rich Ruler having courage to make a change and risk his track record of success.

The Rich Ruler is a Pharisee. His strong suit is compliance. Jesus sets out a path of action that fits in perfectly with the man's strengths.

He gives him a clear instruction: to sell everything he has, give the money away, and follow Jesus. Jesus knew that this option would deliver the man into a place where his "god of self" would lose the compelling evidence of its value. Can you see the kindness in Jesus' plan? Jesus knows that without his "stuff," this Rich Ruler could break free and choose Jesus. Jesus' strategy was designed to kindly remove a barrier to this young man's courage to act on his spiritual recognition of Jesus. Unfortunately, this time, the man chooses to remain "locked up."

The disciples react. Has Jesus laid out a prescription? Is this another "law"? Are people with possessions precluded from life with God? The disciples, too, are familiar with compliance. They ask in verse 26 "*Who then can be saved?*" In Mark 10:27, Jesus replies, saying something that is usually translated as, "*With men it is impossible, but not with God; for with God all things are possible.*" If we look at the Greek language, we see this could be better translated: "Alongside and in close proximity to man, people are in a vulnerable, disempowered condition, but close up with God, and in alignment with Him, people are mighty and effective."

In other words, the Operating System of Judgment aligns a person with themselves, and makes them vulnerable to the values of that operating system and vulnerable to schemes of evil. If a person chooses to walk closely with God, they will value, first and foremost, the connection to God. That makes them powerful. Earthly things, such as money, do not have the power to enslave someone whose foundation is their connection to God.

> *If a person chooses to walk closely with God, they will value, first and foremost, the connection to God.*

The young man originally wanted to know how to get into the Kingdom of Heaven. What Jesus was offering him was already inside him. (Luke 17:21: *"For indeed the Kingdom of God is within you."*) Somewhere inside himself, the man already recognizes Jesus was of God. If the Rich Ruler had been able to let the conviction inside him de-throne the false god of his own mind, he would have come into connection with Jesus and become part of God's Kingdom.

A Third Chance

One of the most beautiful things about this story is seeing how Jesus does not give up. The man chooses to try to qualify himself under the Law. Jesus is undeterred and sets out a course of action in a language that might be acceptable to someone under the law, an opportunity to comply with a clear instruction. Eventually, the man walks away sad, but Jesus does not write him off. Neither does he bait or shame him.

This is not a story about a man who did the wrong thing with Jesus' invitation because he was addicted to money, nor is it a story about a man who did the wrong thing so we can read about him and deduce what the "right thing" would have been. These lenses belong to the Operating System of Judgment. Under the Operating System of Judgment, our understanding of the story is focused on finding a solution to the man's behavior, avoiding the man's mistakes, or developing ways to evaluate the behavior of ourselves or others.

The Operating System of Judgment restricts us from seeing pathways to life that can be broken open by truth (Jesus is the way, the truth, and the life). The Operating System of Judgment wants us to believe we can correctly understand the story and deduce the warning within it. Rather than help us live, that process pre-primes us for condemnation when our own lives fall short. The Operating System of Judgment is an imprisonment system, so it relies on producing outcomes that require compliance, prosper condemnation, or provoke fear.

The Fulfillment

If Jesus had come to teach us "the right thing to do," He would just have given us an expanded version of the Law. Any codebook, even one directly from Jesus Himself, can be fulfilled under the godhead of self, without God. Jesus did not come to expand the Law; He came to fulfill the law. Jesus is called "The Way" because He made a way for us to be the fulfillment of what was in His heart, a way to reclaim what had not existed since the Garden of Eden. He wanted to restore mankind and God walking in union, completely together as one.

This story is about a man who wants connection to Jesus but is locked into a relationship with judgment that bars him from that union. He leaves not yet free. It is also a story about Jesus, our Savior, who is not intimidated by the powers of judgment and never stops opening up the way for people to come into full relational connection to God. Regardless of whether the Operating System of Judgment has made us very wealthy, or if judgment has taken us right to the bottom of the socioeconomic ladder, living the "right way" will do whatever it can to keep us in jail and stop us from enthusiastically telling Jesus that we would like Him to be our source.

Jesus is the Tree of Life. If we choose Him and give our whole selves to our choice, we will be with Him, in a very powerful position (Mark 10:27). Close up with God and in alignment with Him, people are mighty and effective.

Chapter 16

NOT JUST JUDGMENT-FREE

Leaving judgment behind is not an end in itself, but a gateway into a vast lifestyle of infinite possibility where we navigate directly by our connection to God. The object of the transition is not to get to a "judgment-free" life. The object is the realization of the oneness between humanity and God that Jesus prayed for in John 17.

If we have decided to transition our life into the Operating System of Jesus, but are spending most of our time and energy working hard to not judge, perhaps judgment is not disempowered in our life yet. When it is, judgment will become as irrelevant as scuba gear in the middle of a football game. Judgment is not essential equipment and life in God is not enmeshed in it. As we become progressively disentangled, we get on with what God has for us to do. Celebrating non-judgment is not the same as delivering the words and acts of God to the planet. Like sitting in a stationary car and celebrating that we have wheels, celebrating freedom from judgment is a great rip off if we forget to start the engine and experience what our new vehicle can really do.

Experiencing Freedom

Open yourself up to God without measure. It is God's plan for us and it quickly becomes as natural to flow in connection to God as anyone feels that they naturally flow in the million small details of judgment-based decision making. All of the emotions and activities that are involved in a yada relationship within the Operating System of Judgment (torment, endless consideration, analysis, anxiety, cognitive mapping, excitement, strategy development, hypothesizing and speculating, assessment of outcomes, comparison, justification, critique) will, over time, be replaced with the effects of yada with God (increasing understanding, increasing peace, revelation, childlike wonder, access to resilient goodness, delight in God's nearness, selflessness, growth, certainty, safety, divine outcomes).

The transition is a complete remaking of our life. There is no "balanced application" of this teaching, and we do not enter into full relationship with God by navigating a balance between one or another aspect of it. If we are approaching life looking for a balance, or deciding how to prioritize our efforts, then it will be the judge inside of us that decides what the "balanced application" looks like.

That judge is very likely to be advised by a demonic Sanhedrin that will disguise themselves if they have to but will never change their agenda - the undermining of our living connection to God. Leaving behind the "balanced approach" of the Operating System of Judgment, will allow us to live into a real experience of the God who poured out His spirit without measure (John 3:34).

> *Celebrating non-judgment is not the same as delivering the words and acts of God to the planet.*

Increasing Oneness with God

There are some keys that will help a person stay in the forward momentum of the journey into increasing oneness with God. It is important that the journey continues. Re-opening up to judgment, however reasonably the option is presented, will close down life and create discouragement.

To keep moving forward remember:

- You are made you by God, and are ideal for the purposes He has for you. There is a very good fit between you and the expression of knowing God that Jesus wants to come through your life.

- There is much in your natural inclination that is in line with what God wants you to do, so you will accidentally succeed at moving with God more than you might expect.

- Keep living. You and God will together create moments where the connection between you becomes unmistakably clear. If you keep moving forward, more of these anchor points will be created and they will become closer and closer together. Your own history in God will start to propel you forward.

- Divine outcomes will happen in your life.

The mechanism of closing down judgment-based navigation of life is a gateway. It is a key so that a person can walk out of a life-reducing system and lock all the doors behind them as they leave. However, leaving judgment behind is not the destination. The great landscapes of God's personal promised land are waiting for every individual who binds themselves to Him. The goal is a "yada" knowing of God.

If a person is transitioning out from the Operating System of Judgment, the "self" has accepted God's offer to be restored to His original idea. This brings freedom from the weighty burden of ensuring its success without access to infinite knowing. The "self," who up to this point was familiar with operating as the effective godhead, will transition into the security of dependence on God. Letting go of the responsibility the "self" has carried is sometimes a challenge. Familiar with the pattern, a person's spirit can make a new burden of working out how to successfully navigate the Operating System of Jesus before finally releasing governmental responsibility to God.

This book gives minimal illustration of what life looks like when people live from their connection to God. Jesus did not paint people a clear picture of how life would be when they were indwelt by God. Rather, He gave them access points and constant invitations into a real journey. The destination is found in people knowing God. For that, an attachment to His nature has to grow. A growing attachment to God and a spirit recognition of the nature of judgment will grow alongside each other.

As we start to "belong" to God, think His thoughts, and move instinctively with Him, we will also become progressively more and more repelled by judgment. We notice the way it grabs territory and locks down relationships. We start to feel how it is generated by people's godlikeness trying to shore up power over very limited territory.

We begin to feel averse to the impossible burden it puts on us, and the way it causes us to turn in on ourselves. Reflexively, we turn to God when we feel the clutches of judgment trying to reduce life.

- "God, I feel something and I need to know what it is!"

- "God, I don't know what to say in response to that suggestion. Please give me words."

> *The destination is found in people knowing God.*

Parting with Judgment without Judging

As we leave behind the Operating System of Judgment, we do not despise, judge, or label the endeavors we made under that regime when our heart was to earnestly seek God, or to survive as best we could without Him. Even though we can see with hindsight that our gifts and abilities may have been harnessed to promote and support package deals of judgment, those very same gifts and abilities, under the Operating System of Jesus, will be redeployed in their God-appointed purpose.

People who are entangled with the Operating System of Judgment already have to endure several painful dynamics, most painful of all being the practical reality of separation from God. In that separation, it is impossible to imagine what coming more alive to Jesus will look or feel like. If we are living in the Operating System of Judgment, a normal response to a great new idea is to work out how to apply that idea to our lives. This strategy does not work with the Operating System of Jesus.

We cannot aim to successfully carry out a plan to develop "yada" with God. We have to come alive to God. We have to grow a real connection to Father God and stay responsive to His living presence. Release from judgment is a gateway into fuller access to the transforming power of Jesus, but it is not one and the same as being established in God. It is an unlocking tool; a breeze that clears away some smoke so that we can make our way back to the fireplace. It is a life by the fireplace of God's living nearness where we want people to choose to live.

Letting Go of Speculation

Speculation is a judgment-based practice that is particularly hard for people to disentangle from. There are other more overt forms of judgment that are easier to set aside, but under the Operating System of Judgment, speculation has been a needed practice. It is often the backbone of a person's risk management function. Speculation, as a tool, does not sound aggressive or accusatory to most people. Speculative considerations can sound quite gentle. They are not generally experienced as accusing or undermining. If we are familiar with the Operating System of Judgment, speculation can be what we think wisdom sounds like; we may even see it as an essential element of accountability.

We can train ourselves out of relationship with speculation by looking at the underlying assumptions and inferred accusation. This might be a familiar one to some people: *"You better think about doing ………. now. You might need that to keep your options open."* actually means *"You will never know which one missed opportunity will trigger destructive events that you will be powerless to prevent."* The sooner we require the Sanhedrin to voice their "full concern," the sooner we get to hear the life-destroying energy behind speculative consideration and the sooner this form of judgment can be gone from our lives.

God never designed us to live with the infinite uncertainty of speculation. He designed us to be His, to be certain that He will lead us in His path, and to experience the knowing that is part of staying on His unfolding pathway. Our risk management functions are covered by God as part of having our government on His shoulders (Isaiah 9:6).

Peace grows as speculations are silenced. Peace does not mean energy no longer exists; the Kingdom of God is not a place devoid of energy. In fact, there is a "charge" or an energy on everything in the Kingdom. It is perhaps useful to use the analogy of a military campaign. I remember a time when I was a child when my grandmother told me how the Second World War was the most exciting time of her life. She had just wiped tears from her eyes at the memories of loss, but she was real enough to admit that every day seemed to have such importance when the war was on. All relationships seemed heightened, and the whole city she lived in seemed to be galvanized towards one goal.

Realignment

When the living power of God is present in a person's life there are powerful constructive dynamics generated that galvanize and align people. Although the military analogies of religion have grown tired, there is an element to living from our union with God that charges the environment we live in, much like the heightened sensing of a population in times of war. Being part of the advancing governmental structure of God and allowing God to do through us the things that His zeal compels us to do is a vastly different experience of being alive than what people are used to when they navigate under the godhead of self, using the Operating System of Judgment.

Perceptions are different, relationship to time is different, and desires are different. Perhaps we are, in part, breaking open what it means to be "born again." Jesus said that unless this process of being born again happens, we will not enter into the Kingdom of God (John 3:3). Nicodemus, a Rabbi, was shocked, asking how such a thing can be possible. Jesus gave him the following words:

"The wind blows where it wishes, and you hear the sound of it, but cannot tell where it comes from and where it goes. So is everyone who is born of the Spirit" (John 3:8). Again, Jesus highlights to

His Rabbinic friends that they can read the natural systems and the weather but are out of touch with the spirit realm.

As adopted children of God, we have access to beautiful opportunities. God will work through us to heal the sick, cast out darkness, and bring love and hope into dire situations. We become the bridge for the God who lives outside of time, into this earthly reality, inside of time. But, if we are trying to achieve the results that we believe "non-judgment" should look like, we can miss the journey God has for us. Be free to open up to all of what God has for you. Give Him permission to take you deep into what He has for you. He has paid a high price to get you here, and His "mighty right arm" (Psalm 44:3), a vast array of heavenly resources, is devoted to your success.

Chapter 17

GETTING REAL WITH GOD

Most of the limit-setting in theology, church custom, and the personal life of faith are related to fears about what might happen, or what God could require of us if we were actually obedient to Him at His directly-spoken word. The reality of Jesus, the Tree of Life, is so much simpler. The pieces we do not like or understand need to be put on the table. Be real with God and move forward with Him. Jesus has a passion that none would be lost. He makes that point strongly to His Father in John 17.

Our problems and complexities will not destabilize Him. He is supremely competent. His ability makes the process really simple for us. Jesus describes it in Luke 10:27, *"Love the Lord your God with all your heart and soul and mind and strength, and love your neighbor as you love yourself."* That is it. We start with that and let God grow us towards Him. The beauty of the Operating System of Jesus is that we no longer have to complicate the process with our judgments, opinions, and reviews.

Because the planet is now living in the zero-judgment environment of God's mercy, we do not need to be afraid to admit faults or problems. For example, if we do not love God with all our heart, mind, soul, and strength, but we want to, we simply talk to God about it. We might ask Him how we could grow in this direction. We might ask Him if He thinks we don't love Him enough. Perhaps, we keep it very simple and ask Him why our love for Him is the way it is.

205

Getting Real with God

When we look sideways for the purpose of judging ourselves, we look away from Him, and something else that is less than Him becomes our benchmark. When we do this, our judgments haul us back to captivity. We must stay free to be completely real and known by God.

> *He is not threatened by our honesty, nor will He close Himself off to us.*

Praying with people, sometimes for an extended time, as God encounters them, can be powerfully transformational. We take care to allow God to lead them through whatever experience He has for them. Most importantly, if someone is taking time to encounter God, they must be real with Him. He is not threatened by our honesty, nor will He close Himself off to us. Being real is a prerequisite to real connection. God meets real people with understanding and comfort, never condemnation.

Breaking Shame

I went into prayer with a man who had an issue with shame. Like most people who carry shame, he had accidentally formed beliefs about its power to hurt him and to dictate what he did and did not deserve. This is an example of a deeply-held judgment described in an earlier chapter. I asked God to meet us. Jesus came into the room and they started talking together. At the beginning of the encounter, the man would not let Jesus remove his shame. He did not believe Jesus could effectively and permanently do that. This belief formed his anchoring judgment: shame is more powerful than Jesus.

The encounter with Jesus continued. From what I could tell, the man went back to a time when his personal boundaries were transgressed and shame was painted on his soul. He told me later in the prayer time that Jesus invited him to play the game, Monopoly. Suddenly, the man who needed to be set free said, "Oh!" really loudly. I asked what was happening. "Jesus told my shame to go to jail. He told it to go directly to jail, and not to pass go, and not to collect two hundred dollars and not to come back."

Jesus released that man into freedom from shame. Disabling, intrusive night terrors were resolved quickly after a lifetime of tormented sleep.

Shame is the emotional distress of being personally associated with harmful behavior. Isaiah 54:4-5 tells us when we are in the state of marriage-type union with God, we will not be ashamed; however, shame continues to be a big problem for people. God's nature is to cover shame and remove it from us (Isaiah 61:7a). He is the only one who can remove shame. Stuck in the Operating System of Judgment, trying to operate out of our own abilities without Him, we try to behave as He would towards shame. Just as Adam and Eve made themselves clothes out of fig leaves, we act out some form of covering, even if it is a "cover-up." But without Him, we are powerless to get rid of the shame, so the distress is covered up and pushed into secrecy. The problem is not effectively dealt with.

People need encouragement to believe that God can handle the truth. Yes, you can tell God how you really feel if He did not stop you from being hurt or abused when you were a kid. Yes, you can tell God how lonely and betrayed you felt when your husband walked out. Yes, you can tell God you are offended that He didn't bring you a husband or wife. He is ready to hear about it.

Despite the fact that it is impossible to keep secrets from God, many of us have things we think God can't handle, or won't help us with. What does that show us? It shows us how our judgments about the strength of those problems, and our judgments about God and ourselves, have created an unreality. We need to connect with *this* unchanging reality; God is bigger than any situation we have to face. Once we are prepared to take the risk that God can handle ALL our "stuff," we discover that God really is El Shaddai, the all sufficient One (Genesis 17:1). He is God. He can handle anything. He will not cut us off. He will show us the way He has for us.

> *People need encouragement to believe that God can handle the truth.*

God has ways of leading us to get real. He is so jealous for connection that if we decide to disconnect from Him to hide feelings we believe are not "appropriate," we won't find Him in any new life we try to build on a cover-up.

Leanne's Story

Leanne worked as a youth pastor for three years, feeling increasingly discouraged with each passing year. Other staff seemed to have more effective ministries, so Leanne blamed all of this on her personality. She also noticed that she had become increasingly frustrated and resentful of her colleagues who were more outgoing and charismatic than she was.

"How do you honor the fruit of your pastoring?" I asked. "Well...." she drawled quietly, "I suppose when you have the personality I have, and because I am the one that has to keep everything running.

I suppose less is possible." I tried to gently turn the discussion around to resentment, feeling that it was a strong dynamic in her heart. That idea did not resonate with her, but she did admit that God felt far away; she could not access Him at all.

> **God has ways of leading us to get real with Him.**

She wanted to pray and as we did, she saw herself working on very fine needlework. Jesus came near her and was fascinated with what she was doing. She surprised herself when she hid what she was doing from the curious Jesus who wanted to watch. Three times Jesus tried to peek past the hand that she was using to hide her work. Three times she yelled at Him to keep away. Jesus then asked why she was trying to hide it. At first she told Him she wanted it to be a surprise, but Jesus kindly persisted asking her for the real answer.

Leanne suddenly snapped and screamed at Jesus: "Because this is too hard for me and because I hate embroidery and because my hands are too big for this fine kind of work, and if you really wanted me to do this you would have given me smaller hands. You are unkind thinking this is funny. It is not. It is cruel and I don't like you one bit."

Exposing what she felt she had to hide from Jesus, was the beginning of her reconnection to Him. It was the beginning of Leanne becoming vulnerable to God and Him becoming powerful for her. She was not able to live powerfully with God because her judgment caused her to be utterly disconnected from Him.

The woman caught in adultery had a whole lot of stuff she would have liked to hide from Jesus (John 8). When it was exposed by the Pharisees, there was a really good outcome for her. She was the one who received the intimate encounter with Jesus. He wrote life-giving words in the dirt and locked eyes with her, pouring love and light into all the places previously filled with self-loathing. The accusers who wanted her to be judged and punished, were the ones who did not do well that day.

Complete transparency before God, including our sin and our flaws or vulnerabilities is a prerequisite to getting a real encounter with a real God. If we invite Him into our real here-and-now, He does what He promised us He would do; He will meet us there (John 14:23).

If we stay in a direct relationship with God Himself, our problems are not to be feared, they are just "topics for discussion." Is there "room for improvement?" Your God is the same as the God of King David. He is long suffering, slow to anger, and His mercies are new every morning (Lamentations 3:23). The way He covers our inadequacies with His capacities and His superior nature is so good that it inspires us to lay all of our humanity before Him.

How God handles one problem will encourage us to come to Him with the next. We are children of a kind and constructive Father, and He can handle all our doubts, fears, inadequacies, and problems. He understands all of the structures that authored them. As we become "poor in spirit," we discover the path of life that God has for us and we inherit the Kingdom (Matthew 5:3).

Chapter 18

WHAT IS THE FAITH LIFE?

The nature of God is woven into the fabric of this planet through our lives by our faith. It is by faith that we live in His love and allow His thoughts and words to impact ourselves and those around us. Faith is not a mysterious, unfathomable substance. It is a building material. Hebrews 11:1 says, "*Faith is the substance of things hoped for....*"

When a person deliberately chooses to walk on the pathway of growing in faith, they become a person of faith, a person who functions differently because they know their heart is held by God. Know Him and you will have faith. Faith is how you will think and believe and the foundation of all your hopes and ideas when you take the time to get to know God.

A Life of Faith

The faith life is anchored in love. We need to be established in the knowledge that God is love, and that God's heart toward mankind is loving-kindness. Why? Because any other nature cannot be trusted, and, if we try to trust a god who does not love us relentlessly and unconditionally, our faith will be a performance, mostly done to convince ourselves that we have faith.

Trying to convince ourselves that we have faith is not a good idea. We want a living faith so that the spirit realm is compelled to respond. Jesus is well known to have said in Matthew 17:20: "*...for assuredly, I say to you, if you have faith as a mustard seed, you will say to this mountain, 'Move from here to there,' and it will move; and nothing will be impossible for you.*"

We are not called to debate theology or how Christianity should be lived in the modern world. We are called to move the mountains of darkness, and for that we need to understand and grow faith.

For some people, faith implies unreasonable hope, or having to live in denial in the face of desperate circumstances. For others, "living by faith" describes a lifestyle with no source of reliable income. While God can and does meet needs in miraculous ways, faith does not require that we give up paid employment so that God can compel someone else to bring us our daily bread, nor does it require us to be dishonest with ourselves about the extent of challenges we face. A "leap of faith" often describes a presumption that we can embark on some grand scheme without any resources, hoping God will bless the enterprise because we believe what we are doing will benefit Him.

> *We are not called to debate theology or how Christianity should be lived in the modern world.*

It is entirely possible to combine great passion for God and love for His people and the planet with a passionate commitment to moving forward in a way that is inadvertently anchored into the Operating System of Judgment, locking us out of the fruit available if we operate the way Jesus did. Our love for God may be real, but the Operating System of Judgment can lock Him out of our endeavors.

Some people think that having faith means you are brave enough to keep believing the right beliefs about God until you die and are rewarded by getting to Heaven. The powers at work inside the Operating System of Judgment always conspire to reduce faith to an intense commitment to some part of the structure of the jail - A commitment to a particular way forward, a particular expression of who we are, or a particular static belief. A person who lives a life of faith and stays connected to God is something completely different.

What is Faith?

Faith is part of the nature of God. When we encounter God and His love nature, we trust him. Trusting children give themselves to the parent they know they can trust. Trust is a deep foundation to the life of "living by faith." Faith is a substance we live in, so we can manifest God's purposes. It is not a label we should give to a lifestyle of disconnection and uncertainty. Faith opens up brilliant possibility. Faith is an assurance that increases with intimacy. Our trust in God leads to a powerful and ongoing connection so we know that we hear Him and know we can be moved by Him. The assurance that comes when He has something for us to say or do is our faith.

Children of God who have transitioned their whole hearts into Him experience life differently. We think, do, and say things that come straight from God. Our conviction that it is safe to trust God has given us permission to throw our hearts into Him and let our consciousness operate out of Him. We do things without reference to the Sanhedrin. We say things without needing to verify them in a concordance. We may think things about situations with a point of view no one else has had before, because we inhabit a state called faith.

Fear causes people to be self-seeking, and self-seeking believers care most about what they get in the long term: Heaven or Hell? Many believers have actually been taught that this issue is the whole point. God is after much more. He is jealous for relationship. He is driven to connect. He wants to be known by us. The destination is a by-product. Salvation is the by-product of His love. It is the knowing (yada/union) that releases His breath into us and causes the salvation.

If we do not *know* Him, how are we sure we can trust Him? Without trust, what is faith? Without faith, we cannot live in Him, we cannot love Him, we cannot do and say what He is doing and saying. Do you see where this is going? Yada knowing of God is the only option. Intimacy gives us access to a life-long encounter with His nature (love), and that positions us to be effective sons and daughters. There is no substitute for being up close and personal.

The faith life is a beautiful, empowered life. It is a life that leads a person through every situation with a burning power inside their belly. That power becomes their constant courage and says, "*I am infinitely suited to the life I am in now. Before time began, I was designed to be released into this time, with a connection to a God who is infinitely able. Out of His strength, I can extend arms of infinite love. Those touches of His strength are the pathway for a wisdom that is greater than me, and a resurrection power that is greater than death.*" This is a strong way to live.

> *The faith life is a beautiful, empowered life. It is a life that leads a person through every situation with a burning power inside their belly.*

Joseph's Story

A friend brought a man to me for counsel. He was a very successful businessman, but his life was plagued by illness and his family was getting worn out from years of troubles of one kind or another.

The man told me how it had all started five years ago when he had seen some rock climbers climbing up a sheer cliff face. At that time, he felt challenged that he could make a choice (direct his own self): either he could live what he considered (judged) a "comfortable, normal life" or he could "scale great heights"(who would judge which ones, when and how?) for God. As he meditated on the cliffs and mountains he could climb "for God," he concluded this would be the path of greatest heavenly reward.

He said he chose to become "radical." Inside his heart, he made a commitment to the idea of a "mountain climb" straight up a vertical cliff. He envisioned a castle at the top, full of treasure. That choice, to be the self-appointed hero in a God-dedicated thriller cost his family dearly, and portrayed life with God as something frightening to His children.

The life of faith, that takes us out of the role of hero, lets God take center stage and allows us to live in God's certainty. We get to be His friends and live, guided by Him, into His great plans. The life of faith is not about recklessness or risk.

Even Small Faith

Remember that a drop of faith can move a mountain. The slightest breath of faith in a great God can move Him to move anything on our behalf. If our faith does not feel like a powerful and effective position of authority in God, then we have not developed a strong heart connection with God yet, or we are still building a history out of our relationship with His voice. Perhaps we don't have any faith at all yet. It is all a great place to begin. We can honor the connection we have and invite God to take us on a journey of increasing faith.

There is no plan in the heart of God to be impossibly obtuse so that people must spend their lives painfully scratching their way toward faith. His way is beautiful, powerful, and He is zealous to perform it (Isaiah 9:7). Doubt, hesitation, negative speculation about our future, or suggestions of vain hope and romantic labels of disconnection, such as "the dark night of the soul," all belong to the Operating System of Judgment. A heart that is courted by God gets the chance to meet Him. Every heart of every person ever created is courted by God, so no matter how hesitant our "yes" to His pursuit, we are choosing the opportunity to let go of governing ourselves and be adopted into His superior system.

A theologian once described the faith life as a daily struggle to hold onto a truth that we have chosen even though it can't be seen and is intangible in this life. This description is not life-giving, nor is it what God intended us to bear. "Daily struggle" would set us on a path away from faith by ascribing value to the suppression of certainty. It would be preferable to acknowledge our uncertainty before God so He can meet us and grow us toward certainty.

Our connection with God is called faith. As obvious as an ambassadorial cavalcade driving through a derelict city is the person of faith whose heavenly truth goes before, around, and behind them. Faith may be a choice, and it may start small, but it becomes a surrounding force. Like everything in God, if we yield to the heart of Jesus, infinite union with the Divine unleashes its own unlimited, unrelenting power.

Chapter 19

LIVING UNOFFENDED

James 5:9 states: *"Do not grumble against one another, brethren, lest you be condemned. Behold, the Judge is standing at the door!"* The connection between taking offense, "being hurt," and judgment is immediate. It always comes with a "knock on the door" which can be identified as an opportunity to engage judgment and recommence our own incarceration. Remember how closely they are linked. Jesus said: *"Agree with your adversary quickly, while you are on the way with him, lest your adversary deliver you to the judge, the judge hand you over to the officer, and you be thrown into prison"* (Matthew 5:25). Offense leads us back to judgment and puts us back in jail.

Children of God, as agents of light in this world, get the enormous privilege of intimacy with God. Whatever measure of that intimacy we have, *"living water"* (John 7:38) flows out of us into the people around us. This living water may be encouragement, love, inspired wisdom, miracles, honor, or any expression of the vast array of tools and gifts God has given us. All of these things become bridges people can walk across from darkness into light. Offense cuts off this pathway. The bridge is out. Instead of being a bridge into the way of eternal life for people around us, we become isolated in a place of pain.

> *Offense leads us back to judgment and puts us back in jail.*

Defining Offense

So, what is offense and why do we get entangled in it? We define offense as: *The hostile heart response of a person towards the perpetrator of an unjust act against a person or situation.* An alternative definition could be: *The hostile heart response towards any action that causes harm or does not comply with hopes, expectations, or belief of what is "right."*

Offense under the Operating System of Judgment

Under the Operating System of Judgment, people direct themselves even though they may be committed to beliefs and ideas about God. In that context, emotional responses to negative situations are taken as "truths" that are used to decide on a course of action. The Operating System of Judgment inspires a search for how justice can be effected.

Offense under the Operating System of Jesus

Under the Operating System of Jesus, negative emotional responses are "inputs" rather than "truths." These "inputs" are immediately referenced to God through the connection that we keep open. We maintain awareness, not of our human emotional response, but of the connection to God. When we take our earthly emotional inputs to that heavenly setting, we receive living truths from God. We use these living truths, rather than our own emotional responses, to direct us. With heavenly resources, we are recommissioned into the earthly situation to release God's plans and power and see situations of darkness or disappointment be overturned by God's superior realities. We are not agents of earthly justice; rather we provide a release of heavenly life and love.

Richard's Story

Richard complained angrily, "I came home to find that she had done hours of housework and cleaned the tiles throughout the whole house. I was livid. She would never spend that much time on me." After twenty five years of a hostile marriage, Sally could do nothing right in Richard's eyes. Several years of counseling got them nowhere, and they were both desperate.

Richard was offended by how little interest Sally had in him. She didn't do the behaviors he felt he needed from her to make him feel loved.

They both felt like their marriage was nearing the end of the road. I prescribed a behavior that would give Richard a chance to experience the Operating System of Jesus in his marriage. I told him to ban himself from speaking to his wife unless he got words from God for her, and to ban himself from believing any thoughts or emotions he had towards her unless he felt certain that they were from God.

Evidently things shifted when God reminded Richard how blessed he was to have one of God's daughters taking care of his home. One month later, they both felt hope for their marriage and their behaviors that compounded pain had stopped altogether. One year later, they said they were happy in marriage for the first time in 25 years.

> ***We are not agents of earthly justice; rather we provide a release of heavenly life and love.***

Why is being offended such a problem?

1. In judging the perpetrator, we step outside of mercy. All judgment was given to Jesus and paid for by Him.

2. In positioning ourselves as judge, we lose access to the redemptive eyes of Jesus.

3. Having lost our ability to see redemptively, we cannot partner with Jesus.

4. Our anger is based on our faith in someone else's darkness. If we stay connected to God we cannot be that impressed by their failings.

Judgment leads to storing up attitudes in our hearts that are completely outside the love and mercy of God. The appetite of those attitudes is for justice and retribution. Retribution would argue, "*Something wrong has happened so someone has to pay.*" It also has various hidden forms that sound more like "*I am going to give you an opportunity to take responsibility for the pain your words have caused.*" This is justice, revenge, or paying the penalty for evil. This is the very appetite Jesus fulfilled on the cross. To practice it is to declare to the spirit realm that we consider His death of no effect.

Jesus is the way, the truth and the pathway to life. Choosing to be unoffendable will help us to stay on His pathway, releasing His life and being refilled by Him. No matter what operating system the other person uses, we ask God for insight to see the original hope, or the stolen hope expressed by their behavior. Maybe consider it like this, "*If that person had felt powerful, loved, and connected to God, what would they have chosen to do instead?*" This is a great stop check when we could otherwise allow ourselves to be hurt by someone else's behavior. If we are not available for offense, our understanding positions us to become agents of redemption. If we practice operating like this, avoiding offense becomes simple:

• See the heart of the person who has committed the offensive behavior. Ask God to let you in on the person's hopes no matter how distorted their actual behavior may have been. The job of a daughter or son of God is not to assess or judge behaviors, but to see into their heart and find the pathway to greater freedom for that heart.

• Stay seated in heavenly places (Ephesians 2:6). If we retain an operational awareness of our proximity to Jesus, we expect inputs of a heavenly nature and believe less easily in our own emotional thinking. We are not in egalitarian relationship with broken situations. We never need to believe we are on the same level. We can always choose for our involvement to be *from* our position in God.

• Stay nimble, moving with the light even as evil schemes try to lock you down. Let the clothing of God keep you slippery as the tendrils of entrapment try to grab at your heart, mind, or words, asking you for allegiances and commitments that will pull you out of freedom.

When we are on a forward journey into greater intimacy with God, offense is always looking for an opportunity to take us out of our forward journey and replace it with a static position, usually head-to-head with something that is "wrong." Our choice is to remain seated in heavenly places with God (Ephesians 2:6), connected to what our heavenly Father is doing.

Chapter 20

INHABITING PEACE AND BECOMING PEACEMAKERS

Isaiah chapter 9 describes the coming of Jesus the Messiah and the dramatic change in the spiritual ordering of the planet that would take place. Jesus would initiate an ever-increasing state of peace driven forward by nothing less than the zeal of God.

> *The people who walked in darkness have seen a great light; those who dwelt in a land of deep darkness, on them has light shone. You have multiplied the nation; You have increased its joy; they rejoice before You as with joy at the harvest, as they are glad when they divide the spoil. For the yoke of his burden, and the staff of his shoulder, the rod of his oppressor, You have broken as on the day of Midian. For every boot of the tramping warrior in battle tumult and every garment rolled in blood will be burned as fuel for the fire. For to us a Child is born, To us a Son is given; And the government shall be upon His shoulder, And His name shall be called Wonderful Counselor, Mighty God, Everlasting Father, Prince of Peace. **Of the increase of His government and of peace there will be no end,** on the throne of David and over His kingdom, to establish it and to uphold it with justice and with righteousness from this time forth and forever more.*

Verse 2: Jesus is the light of the world. He came to reveal the hidden things of God, those we were too far away from Him to see clearly. And they are now ours as His children.

Verse 3: Jesus came so we could have "abundant life." He came to bring us joy, and sufficiency—as on the day of harvest when there is more than enough.

Verse 4: Under the Old Covenant, life was subservient to the Law. Rods, staffs, and yokes are symbols of authority. The "staff of his shoulder" is a reference to the authority and the dominion of a person. In the Hebrew, "shek·em" (shoulder) can also refer to a tract of land or a territory; in other words, the extent of a person's domain. People were given no choice under the Old Covenant. Their lives were under the oppression of the Operating System of Judgment. They were under the law. There was no freedom. There was no possibility to be an integrated part of God's being.

All dominion except God's is broken with the coming of the Messiah. Jesus brought a complete change in the spiritual authority structure. He lifted the heavy burden of not only external government and law off the backs of people, but also the burden of navigating our own selves through the journey of life. We can now choose to let God replace all that with His own infinitely good and wise authority.

Verse 5: Jesus brings a way to end warring and conflict. We can let the "Prince of Peace" (Isaiah 9:6) rule in our affairs.

Verse 6: The government is on *His* shoulder now, not ours. He is our all-sufficient guide for life, our strength and position of power, our protection and our place of peace.

Verse 7: There is no end to Jesus' story. Whatever temporary advances evil appears to make, the power and authority of God, and the peace that He brings with it, will only increase. The *zeal* of God is behind this!

> *This is the will of the Lord and He is zealous to perform it.*

God's Domain

The change in the governmental history of the world described in Isaiah 9, when Jesus' death made union with Father God possible, opened the way for us to relinquish our independent operation and be adopted into God as sons and daughters. The power working through us can now be God's direct dominion - the darkness-into-light, life-transforming power of God Himself. All people who join together in this way become a corporate extension of God. They become His Bride, the longed for consummation of God's love. All of the beings through whom God's dominion is operating, and all of the territory under their government is the domain of The King, God's Kingdom. All of us in the Kingdom operate under this spiritual force - the authority of God. It is this direct authority on our lives that compels darkness away from us, causing us to experience peace.

The Kingdom of God on earth exists from the time of Jesus and expands forever until the history of the planet ends. Every person who trades in their limitations as an independent person for the surpassing ability available through personal connection to God, becomes part of the Kingdom. Inside this Kingdom of God, no matter what our situation, we will have arrived there with Him, and will be fully empowered and resourced there by Him.

Nothing about our future is ever at stake. It is the position described in Isaiah 33, and the one asked for by Jesus in John 17; a position so secure in its ordination from God, that we are fully able to give our whole selves to any other being on God's behalf. Peace and God's government makes us a strong and secure conduit for the advancing dominion of God.

Romans 8 describes the process and the security that people living into their connection with God enjoy as He works His purposes through them. We read a powerful statement in verse 28, "*And we know that all things work together for good to those who love God, to those who are the called according to His purpose.*" Those who are devoted, but tricked away to answer the call of the other operating system, are not inside of the all-encompassing protection of God as He zealously achieves His will.

In verses 33 and 34, we are given permission to disallow the Sanhedrin to accuse us, to prevent ourselves from being condemned to the jail. "*Who shall bring a charge against God's elect? It is God who justifies. Who is he who condemns? It is Christ who died, . . .*" Any scheme that wants to undermine the peace of God's children has to find a way to trick us so it can pull us out of our connection with God and back into the self-reliance of the Operating System of Judgment.

> *Nothing about our future is ever at stake with God.*

Transition into Jesus

As our transition into the Operating System of Jesus progresses, more and more of our history will be built out of our intimate connection to Him. Even our possessions will have "God stories" attached. The details of our lives will, in greater measure, reflect the sublime strength of God's plans and purposes. It is a great blessing to have God remove our peace substitutes, and replace them with peace, intimate connection, and increasing demonstrations of His power.

As people set out on the journey, disentangling from the tendrils of the Operating System of Judgment and learning how to access the resources and strengths of God, can be difficult. There is a detoxification phase. There are several dynamics in the transitional stages that can destabilize people, causing people to question their commitment to the Operating System of Jesus.

Letting our lives come into peace as we are established in the way of Jesus gives us a powerful foundation in God. People who are transitioning into the Operating System of Jesus and shedding anxiety, insecurity, or torment as they discover peace, sometimes report an initial season of euphoria. The euphoria comes as an expression of relief, that the painful dynamics of the old operating system are gone. As the euphoria subsides, if God manifests as a stillness, some people confuse this with absence. He is not absent, but neither is He competing as a "stimulus" with all of the other ideas and stories trying to convince the new inhabitant of peace that life with God will disappoint. Peace can initially seem too quiet and too still. But God may wish to have us acclimate to it. In God's peace there is:

- No chorus of accusation

- No threats

- No excitement "on tap"

- No adrenaline from alluring fantasy.

People may be able to live without one of these, but observationally, the absence of all four is very uncomfortable for most people. This is the challenge of the detoxification phase. People may feel an instinct or may come under social or spiritual pressure to take the reins back into their own hands.

226

This instinct needs to be resisted so that the recalibration of all our senses can be completed by God.

Learning to inhabit peace requires a transition where we cancel our dependence on false sources of life and stimulation, and learn how to perceive God. Once we are weaned away from the stimulation of the stories and ideas we subscribed to under the Operating System of Judgment, and have learned to inhabit peace, our relationship with God will start to become richer and more real to us. Our emotions will recalibrate to the movements of God.

In the Operating System of Jesus, inspiration from God compels people to do what God has for them to do. In the Operating System of Judgment, burdensome layers are added which combine to produce an unhealthy forward pressure to achieve. The Operating System of Judgment applies moral, economic, and social imperatives to life to create drive. History is mined for its resource of stories about people who have "succeeded" or "failed" depending on whether the effect desired is to rev people up or terrify them forward. The focus of this way of living becomes learning and striving today so that we can succeed tomorrow in a way that we could not in the past.

It wasn't like this for Jesus, and it is not supposed to be like this for us either. The past belongs to history and the future belongs to God. He has told us to leave it to Him (Matthew 6:34). The fruit of doing so is profound. If we do not allow preconceptions, assumptions, judgments, and rationalizations about the past or tomorrow to create a demand on our idea of **now**, then the spiritual output of **now** is not stolen by a pre-existing arrangement that we have made to **tomorrow** (horizontally forward), and it is not spiritually answering to a debt that we have believed we have to the **past** (horizontally backwards). This releases all of the spiritual output of today "vertically" to God. This is worship.

Jewish culture has always included this sense that everything we do is supposed to be worship, but Western Christianity has not known how to achieve this. This state of being connected to Him, and not bound to the past nor the future, is how we give Him everything that we are. This gives the full potential of our activities to God as worship, and allows us to be completely available to know and receive from Him. The spiritual output of our lives is directed towards God, and God is directed towards the planet through us. This is the place of peace.

The system inherited from the Tree of the Knowledge of Good and Evil works hard to engage people in the forward pressure. It encourages people to make what is effectively a covenant of some sort or other with that pressure so that they are never released from it. It is a very powerful way to make sure that people never get to know God in a deep intimate way, and never live in peace.

> *The past belongs to history and the future belongs to God.*

Jesus did not subscribe to anything in any way that would cause His life to come under the forward pressure of the Operating System of Judgment. He was able to stay completely with God, and all of the output of His life was deployed towards the living purposes God was working towards at the time.

We are supposed to remain free in the same way that Jesus was, but such divinely-empowered freedom is not common among people. That is because the Operating System of Judgment works to entangle even those who would resist the dominant pressures. There are a great many people who feel some sense of darkness in the pressure of the Operating System of

Judgment. Western culture does offer an amazing array of "rewards" to individuals willing to subscribe, but it also exposes one's life to a drivenness that is genuinely painful to people who have the gift of spiritual discernment.

People trying to escape the pressure of the operating system have sought time-and-time again to create a nirvana, or some sort of theological utopia. But such a search wrongly pairs the pain with hard work. Work is one of the great opportunities of life on earth, and, when we are deployed by God into the work He has for us, it is a source of great satisfaction. The pain in life under the Operating System of Judgment is because of what is authoring the pressure. These lives are harnessed to serve an operating system that keeps people away from God. Those who feel the pressure and decide to resist are encouraged to reform, present a radical alternative, or anything at all that is *still* defined by its relationship to the great network of spiritual constriction built out of the Operating System of Judgment. If we can be persuaded to believe in the "stance" we take **relative** to the mainstream of pressure, then we will remain spiritually entangled.

Many people live with great pressure to serve God in a certain way or to a certain measure because of judgments about what it looks like to fulfill the Great Commission (Matthew 28:18-20). The Operating System of Judgment always creates a justification for the forward pressure, and will resort to using the Great Commission as a source of pressure if it has to.

God encourages us repeatedly instead to stop still and seek Him:

Be still, and know that I am God; I will be exalted among the nations, I will be exalted in the earth! (Psalm 46:10)

229

The line translated "Be still and know that I am God" is really only three words: *Raphah yada Elohiym*. A paraphrase would be *"Drop out, let go, fall away from that into deep intimate union with God."* The result, as described in the next two lines of the psalm, will be that God will be known and made famous throughout all the earth if we do. He tells us that if we detach from the system that promises so much but locks us down into its constrictions, we will come into a knowing of Him and He will become known throughout the whole earth. Setting ourselves free into living out of our connection to God will achieve what our well-intentioned strategies will not.

For example, if we decide that NY City needs a slow-food movement, and we set that as our goal, then our success will provide great moments of relief for New York City, but we will not set the city free from the pressure the operating system has it under. We will probably become very busy helping the city learn how to do slow food well. In the same way in church life, if a group gives itself to a specific correction or reformation, for example: "more accurate Bible teaching" or "more Holy Spirit" or "more access to spiritual fathers," that group will have positioned itself relative to the dominant culture built from the Operating System of Judgment and will be entangled back into the operating system.

This will bring the whole group under pressure and few will access peace. Only recommissioning our lives into the Operating System of Jesus will position us in the "blue sky" space of Jesus where we are fully His and He is completely available to us. This is the powerful landscape of peace from which the stories of God and His children go out into all the earth and make Him known.

Relieving Pressure

Real separation from the pressure of the operating system is possible. Not as a disenfranchised, marginalized state, but as an empowered freedom to live with full access to the resources and timing of God. That is peace. Separated from the entanglements of the Operating System of Judgment, we let the government of life rest on His shoulders rather than ours. With Him, we get to rebuild the ruined cities that lie decimated by the unfulfilled promises of the Operating System of Judgment. Peace is a spiritual result of the process of growing our life into God.

God is completely able to live Himself out through us into the planet, and we are fully able to access God so that all our yearnings are fully accommodated by His infinite capacity and resources. In this context, our lives are available to be fully commissioned by God into the work He has for us to do. Many reach old age without ever touching this level of opportunity for fulfillment.

The importance of peace in the Kingdom of God cannot be overstated. **Advancing** in love and overcoming all evil is God's preferred way to **maintain** peace. The greatest power of all will be at work around us and through us as we live in peace. The powers of darkness recognize when people are fully equipped to carry out what God is asking of them and know if they are not distracted into the Operating System of Judgment, they will succeed. In peace, we advance successfully under the cover of God. This is God's perfect model and the reason for the inseparable link between peace and advancement.

Building Peace

The foundation of a believer's ability to live in peace is humility. Any connection with all-powerful God engages two forces that work to cause humility. One is the surpassing greatness of God. He is infinitely powerful and, by contrast, we are quite small. Real connection with Him keeps this reality alive. The second force that constantly provokes humility is the unlimited possibility of connection with God. No matter how "connected" to Him we believe we are, He is infinite. The need for God in the world is constant, so as long as we are alive, life itself will reinforce how much God is needed.

People who live in intimacy with God and are always ready to grow in their connection to God cause peace. No matter their situation, whether things work out "successfully" or not, children of God make peace. It is the normal spiritual result of people living out of the Operating System of Jesus. Jesus is *"the Prince of Peace"* (Isaiah 9:6).

By contrast, any practitioner of the Operating System of Judgment is unknowingly set up to create conflict. The governmental conditions of the Operating System of Judgment are fractured and insecure. Here is why:

- Every person in the Operating System of Judgment is their own governor; therefore, every person is an independent government.

- None of those governments are connected directly to the zeal of the Lord to achieve His purposes. In the spirit realm, God's purposes are sure and nothing else is; thus, other governmental systems are extremely insecure. They are constantly looking for ways to demonstrate power and validity.

232

- Every point of connection between separate domains is a clash of self-interested governments that can only be resolved through negotiation or displacement of the competing government. Every governing entity outside of the Kingdom of God is constantly trying to shore up and protect its powerbase.

Advancing in love and overcoming all evil is God's preferred way to maintain peace.

Disconnected from the certainty, authority, and the infinite ability of God, every moment in the Operating System of Judgment is assessed for its potential impact on the powerbase of the false godhead. Negotiation in that insecure context is compelled towards self-interest. Even when the overt agenda is for the good of all, the self-interest will be expressed as a subconscious commitment to the judgments that form a person's view of what reality is. Brokering self-interest will be the hallmark of solution-finding in the Operating System of Judgment. People are not able to live without codes to organize how self-interest is managed. They are constantly compelled to re-legitimize their own power, ability, needs, and direction.

Under the Operating System of Judgment, the world is perceived to be populated by enemies and allies.

Jesus gave us a way to live that empowers us to love our enemies because there is no enemy that can be a threat to God. Under the Operating System of Jesus, conflict is disempowered. Conflict requires at least two parties to energize it. The person who is allowing God to work through them is never empowered to cause conflict. They are a maker of peace.

It quickly becomes apparent that each great act of violence carried out by people in the name of God since the time of Jesus, required people to step out of what God was actually wanting to do. Such acts of conflict could only happen with great commitment to particular justifications within the unseen cultural captivity of the Operating System of Judgment: harmful fruit of the civilization-wide adoption of this operating system.

> *Peace is a spiritual result of the process of growing our life into God.*

The Medieval Crusades could not have happened without great commitment to belief in the threat of Islam. It would have been impossible for leaders of the Protestant Reformation to set fire to monasteries and enjoy burning monks to death unless they had given their hearts to faith in their "right" application of theology. Only captives can maintain the practice of judgment that is necessary to navigate in the way of violence and death. Strong connection to God will give us great access to His solutions and His solutions result in peace.

In any situation, a person who lives the Operating System of Jesus has one foundational need- to stay connected to God. In the face of a problem, we can maintain that connection as God opens up a pathway of redemption.

> *Strong connection to God will give us great access to His solutions and His solutions result in peace.*

234

<u>Responses that build peace in the context of a problem:</u>

•Know that our connection to God is increasing and includes the possibility of access to infinite wisdom and infinite understanding.

•Stay in the Operating System of Jesus, and find out what God has for us to do and say.

•Watch for a pathway of redemption to open up either directly through circumstances or through an individual's connection to God.

•Do whatever God has commissioned us to do to encourage the adoption of the pathway God is opening up.

> *The connection to God always exists and can always increase; we choose it and tend it.*

As we enter into situations that could involve conflict, we give up our "right" to be right. We surrender that option for the far more powerful opportunity to be a conduit of God. Likewise, if a redemptive solution does not seem to open up, despite our best effort to do what we believe God is doing or saying, we do not drop out of His operating system and back into judgment. We return to God for direction. The connection to God always exists and can always increase; we choose it and tend it. This creates a momentum in the "system" toward redemption and being discipled through every situation by God.

At no point is a human preconception or assessment of a problem invited to govern us. At no point is the achievement of the right outcome a priority over growing in our connection to God, nor is any outcome considered more powerful than connection to God. God's pathway to solutions will be unique to each situation and will always invite both parties closer to God, causing an increase in the expression of righteousness and peace.

How an individual is coerced into conflict by the Operating System of Judgment:

• Assume and accept that access to God and His wisdom and understanding is limited, and assume our expectations and understanding of those limits are "reasonable" or "appropriate" for modern times.

• Revert to what we know and understand to guide us through the situation. (Reinstate the Operating System of Judgment, so we become the godhead and subject to our entire natural limits.)

• Assess the problem and the "threat" posed by the problem.

• Choose the best intervention based on the changes we believe are necessary.

• Present the chosen solution to the person or group we believe are "causing" the problem.

• Try to motivate the people or group to accept the solution to the problem.

From the first step, a person is operating as judge. Once they start choosing and applying solutions, they become the director (or godhead).

Love and life do not flow from spiritual dynamics that reduce connection to God.

Judgment, in this era of mercy, is so spiritually repulsive that only very desperate people will receive interventions and solutions from people who are operating in it. If the solutions we are offering are bringing people into the Operating System of Judgment, people are legitimately better off moving away from us and toward someone else who can connect them to God. Love and life do not flow from spiritual dynamics that reduce connection to God.

Peace In Jesus

The children of God living a life of union with Him make Jesus the cornerstone of God's righteous government and peace on the planet. Peace is what we live in when we choose a lifestyle of closeness, our heart in His. Jesus lived in peace, and His plan is that we do too. As we live out the course of our earthly life with God as the epicenter of everything we do and say, then when we arrive at the end of our time on earth, we transition out of this earthly journey into something that we already inhabit and love - intimate union with God. People who know God know there is no fear in death.

Chapter 21

THE PLANET GETS TO SEE GOD AS HE IS

Human life is the opportunity to navigate a personal story through infinite possibility. We choose to navigate this either with God or without Him. The Operating System of Judgment offers us stories and constructs that come with justification, creating reduced realities that are simple to comprehend and offer us a sense of power, purpose, or control. As much as we allow ourselves to believe in the value of our judgments, we can create and inhabit realities based on them, and use them to chart a course. However, inside the heart of God is the blueprint for each human life. If God is allowed to be who He is, we get to be how He designed us to be. Our humanity connects with His infinite strength, wisdom, and resources. Our life becomes the scribing of His infinite ability into the sands of finite space and time.

Jesus was the highest price God could pay to ensure full connection to the Father is available. His one strongest desire was that we would be one; us in Him and He in us.

We need God. We were born to be His. We want Him close, and we would rather do what He designed us for than anything else. The lifestyle described in *this* book gives God the greatest possible influence over what we do and say, and moves us away from a relationship with judgment.

> *Our life becomes the scribing of His infinite*
> *ability into the sands of our finite space and time.*

The journey is held to account by the fruit it produces (Matthew 7:20). Most of the stories of people doing weird things as they try to live a radical life for God are efforts based on someone's JUDGMENT of what that needs to look like. Such attempts are an effort to live the way of Jesus according to a prescription dictated by the Operating System of Judgment. It is impossible for that to succeed.

Staying Alive to God

Once we experience living out of our direct connection to God, we must not bring judgment back in. Even if all our foundational assumptions are 100 percent correct, we still must not operate as the judge. Operating in 100 percent correct judgment in this era of mercy still puts us in direct defiance of God. So believing we are "right" should be a very uncomfortable position for anyone. The faith communities of Jesus' day (the Pharisees) organized their lives around what they believed was the right thing to do. That was not Jesus' focus.

Jesus was always alive to God. The position of "being right" does not exist in Jesus. In Jesus, we live in truth that is alive and empowered. It destroys darkness and releases life. Our life is positioned in His relentless love, fully resourced to achieve His purposes. Knowing God is our certain foundation. Our confidence is in Him, not in being right, or having a correct stance on an issue. Jesus is the only human being, ever, who had the ability to judge everything completely in line with God's truth. Even He did not operate in judgment. Living in the Operating System of Jesus, we sacrifice the self-serving satisfaction of "being right" to preserve the access we have to the Father and the access He has to us.

> *Jesus was always alive to God.*

Great demonstrations of God's love and His power have always been available, but the Operating System of Judgment is so pernicious, that even these invitational touches of the "above and beyond of God" can be turned into ammunition to prosper "the right thing." Hope for life-giving connection to God morphs into a commitment to a way of doing Christianity, or a cultural application of our ideas about God. Corporately, the body of Christ has glimpsed what is possible, but, with the best intentions, we created new norms and routine behaviors out of what, in its purer form, was access to God.

People touched by God want to know how to live with Him. We cannot just offer them a lifestyle that includes some access to some symptoms of God. If together, we pursue the works of the Holy Spirit, signs, wonders, and prophetic activity, but do not grow into a daily moment-by-moment life with God Himself, we will remain imprisoned on the wrong side of God's invitation. We will take gifts from God's hands as He reaches into our jail, but we won't let Him set us free. Many people look to God's hands for help, but few know how to let Him pull us out of the prisons we have created.

Outside of the system of judgment, we emerge into a beautiful ecosystem: God's personal history with His beloved planet, His desires, His longing, and His commitment to grow up a Bride from all the people on the earth as they respond to the price Jesus paid to bring us all back together, we and the Father as one, just as Jesus and the Father are one (John 17). Whether we are descended from a family line of generations of believers or were adopted minutes ago, all of us are invited to be part of the preparation for a wedding; the consummation of God's love story with the planet.

Jesus demonstrated the simplicity of life in that system. He left us a very simple pattern to follow - to do and say what the Father is doing and saying. He took the system all the way to death so that we could see that in simple obedience and complete union with the Father, even death loses its power.

Individual believers who have given themselves permission to be God's, and operate out of Him, start to develop anchor points of absolute conviction; moments and events when we knew that we knew that we were with God and had spoken His words or done exactly what He had for us to do. We cannot fall further away from God than our anchor points. The more God authors each of our moments, the closer together those anchor points get. Daily moments of connection to God that are clearly from Him make it hard to step off the path God is creating. We will have the courage to walk through any journey because we know that God Himself is writing a story through us. History will tell the story.

> *Daily moments of connection to God that are clearly from Him make it hard to step off the path God is creating.*

Living From Connection

The effectiveness of living from our connection to God stirs great enthusiasm because it sets people free and empowers them quickly. People who are aware of how to move with the manifest presence of God have lives that are dense with demonstrations of His nature. The gospel message does not have to be made appealing because Jesus can be directly demonstrated, and He is appealing beyond anything else.

The God that people connect to is all powerful, perfectly effective to save, and always new. He is the *"Desire of All Nations"* (Haggai 2:7), and we are inextricably joined to Him. Believers experiencing this way of life exist in every nation, living and working in a huge variety of settings, loving people, and using their own personal connection with God as a bridge across which anyone can come to God for themselves. As they share the living connection they have, people are pulled out from despair and torment into the brightness of God's realities.

In union with Jesus, operating as He did with the Father, we will surrender our ability to lock ourselves down and instead lock onto God Himself. The transition will open up an unlimited measure of Him for ourselves and for the planet. The rivers of life and love, and the sheer confidence that pour out of every believer will create an expectation of a highly effective "everyday believer" where once the church only expected the great heroes of the faith to be highly effective in God. Leaders will be the *"under-shepherds"* (I Peter 5: 1-4) who display and teach the one greatest thing of all, how to know God and how to live into ever-increasing knowing of Him.

The planet is weary of the burden of carrying responsibility for things we cannot understand nor influence without God. Throughout history, the pain of mankind's separation from God has provoked people to cry out for God to come close, to end the separation. 750 years before Jesus, Isaiah the prophet cried out to God on behalf of the planet pleading, *"Oh, that You would rend the heavens! That You would come down! That the mountains might shake at Your presence!"* (Isaiah 64:1).

Isaiah cries out for God to make Himself known in a way that is direct, definite, and enduring. A few verses later, he sees into the future to what people will say about life on the earth when God has "come down." He sees people living in a close parent-to-child relationship with God, people as children held in the loving hands of the perfect Father: God: *"But now, O LORD, You are our Father; We are the clay, and You are our potter: We are all the work of Your hand"* (Isaiah 64:8 ESV).

Seven centuries later, this prophecy is fulfilled in Jesus. On the afternoon of the day Jesus was crucified, the sky went dark, there was a terrible sound of thunder, and in the temple in Jerusalem, the curtain that closed off the most Holy Place of God's presence was ripped in two by God. From the top to the bottom, the curtain was torn out of the way. There was no more separation! God ripped open the heavens and came down (cf., Isaiah 64:1).

Extraordinary Access

The earth is now awash with the opportunity to encounter God; an opportunity so extraordinary that our minds cannot comprehend it. It is time for this earth to be a planet of children; children who believe Him and His design for us because this planet was never our idea, it was His. We were never our idea; we are His, so we do not need to carry the burden of trying to make our future conform to our ideas when instead it can become a life of bright and defined anchor points into God for a population cast adrift on an ocean of vagaries and questioning.

Humanity got stuck in an operating system that makes very little of the opportunity to have God. In fact, the Operating System of Judgment is a strategy of darkness to withhold people from God, even the ones who have chosen to love Him. Operating in judgment puts us under pressure to do the exact thing we have chosen not to do. This operating system makes us the servants of another god, the god of self, even when our heart's desire is to live for Jesus. Under the Operating System of Judgment, eyes are veiled to the movement of God on the planet.

The Operating System of Judgment has people scanning relationships for support and agreement, and is content with entwining ideas of God into our ideas of what is right. The living God is not required. Judgment-derived emotions will take empathy from other believers as a sign of connection while children die and believers lose everything at the altar of an absent god who doesn't speak or act.

> *Imagine the compounding of righteousness that could come if a generation lived in unbroken supernatural union with God.*

The Operating System of Jesus

The Operating System of Jesus offers us the opportunity to stay in honor, love, and freedom so all of the great things that can happen through time and unbroken relationship will manifest "naturally" in their God-appointed setting, the global Body of Christ. Imagine the compounding of righteousness that could come if a generation lived in unbroken supernatural union with God. What if judgment did not cause one generation to differentiate itself from the previous generation based on their limitations or perceived failures? What if a whole generation of believers decided they would grow together into a global body that allowed God to determine how and when He was going to manifest Himself through us? We would be known as the people who are like God.

Set free from the insecurity of having to measure or assess our relationships with God, believers could simply honor whatever connection to God they have, and let God lead us all closer to Him. Instead of tending to our inadequacies, we would remain "on call," ready to move on His behalf.

God's children can be the most confident and effective people on earth. Once people understand the power of only doing and saying what Father God has for us to do and say, there will be no need to second-guess God. Jesus told us that the Kingdom of Heaven is inside of us (Luke 17:21). The people who know God will make everything that is within them available to God, to move as He moves, to speak as He speaks. His Kingdom is built as we present everything that is within us to Him and activate the living connection He paid for.

Motivation becomes strong and pure when a person is convinced that they are the home of the living God. They do things because God wants them to, not out of obligation or competition. The conflicted dynamics disappear as people are driven by a clear connection and certainty, by gratitude and by affection for the life of God they know they can trust. Everything Jesus did worked. He was confident and effective.

> *Once people understand the power of only doing and saying what Father God has for us to do and say, there will be no need to second-guess God.*

The Operating System of Jesus is designed to take the limitations of the past and the speculations of the future out of the way so that the surpassing nature and power of God can become the resilient core of our lives now. When God is known and demonstrable, everything is held close to hope. Our absolute assurance becomes more than enough for us.

We become the water that never runs dry (Isaiah 58:11). His supreme sufficiency, His loving kindness, His zeal, His love that is stronger than death, all flow out to the planet through **His** words **we** say, and through **His** miracles that **we** do. The unbroken connection that Jesus paid for allows this flow of love and life to happen.

It was God's longing for connection that put us on the planet. It was His longing for connection that caused Him to brood over His people, waiting for thousands of years because He knew that one day, He would have us back. Ultimately, God showed us that He would not shy away from death if it meant that He could be one with us in the life that is without beginning and without end.

JESUS CHRIST LIBERATOR

www.jesuschristliberator.org

Jesus Christ Liberator is the international ministry of Iain Bradbeer. Iain is highly respected for his ability to access, understand and describe the structural and governmental aspects of the spirit realm that affect every life. Through his writing and public speaking he teaches in an integrated and practical way for both individuals and organizations.

For further teaching and resources or to invite Iain to come and speak to your organization, please visit our website:

www.jesuschristliberator.org

Please share your story of this book's impact, or communicate with the Authors at our book website:

www.theoperatingsystemofjesus.com

Made in the USA
San Bernardino, CA
01 August 2014